BAB
NAMES
2010

Eleanor Turner

white
LADDER

This edition first published in Great Britain 2009 by

Crimson Publishing, a division of Crimson Business Ltd

Westminster House

Kew Road

Richmond

Surrey

TW9 2ND

A catalogue record for this book is available from the British Library.

ISBN 978 1 90541 058 3

Printed and bound by LegoPrint SpA, Trento

Acknowledgements

I would like to extend my utmost gratitude to Cerys Owen, Shelley Heck and Michael Turner for their contributions; without them this book would have been much shorter. My thanks are also given to Beth Bishop at Crimson Publishing for her patience and guidance throughout the project. Finally, the greatest thanks go to Owen Henri Turner, who grew patiently inside me while I wrote this book and waited to be born until I had chosen his name.

A note on how to use this book

While the author and publisher acknowledge that names may vary widely in spellings and pronunciations, names have been arranged by common spellings and first initial only. Alternative first initial spellings are listed under their relative letter, but spelling variations with the same first initial are listed only once, under the most common spelling.

Contents

PART THREE Girls' Names A–Z

With lists of…

Introduction

> **❝** What's in a name? That which we call a rose
> By any other name would smell as sweet.
>
> William Shakespeare, *Romeo and Juliet*
> (Act II, Sc ii) **❞**

Shakespeare may have had it wrong when he wrote those lines. A name *is* important because it is the one thing to stay with your child throughout their entire life and affects who it is they become. Having a name which they can live with and be proud of, therefore, is crucial to having a good start in life and this book will show you exactly how to pick the right one.

Sometimes choosing the right name is simply a case of hearing one you like near the birth of your baby and knowing instantly that you've chosen correctly. However, for the vast majority of parents the naming process becomes a complex minefield of trying to please parents, grandparents, friends and siblings while trying to avoid embarrassing acronyms with their newborn's initials, or names that could be shortened into ridiculous nicknames. Parents also like to choose something unique, but not *too* unique, or common but not *too* common, or a name which is symbolic of a cultural event at the time of the baby's birth. A name could come from

1

an admired celebrity's baby, a sports star, or an influential historical or political figure. It could also come from the family tree, or be part of a long-standing tradition where sons are named after fathers and daughters are named after mothers. The possibilities and chances to make a mistake or offend someone are practically endless and it's understandable that it can set some parents into panic mode.

Well, never fear. This book talks you through each of your options carefully and discusses how to solve your baby-naming dilemmas in practical ways. It's also updated annually, which means you'll know the latest trends in baby names and find out the most popular names for your baby's classmates to help guide you towards your final decision. If you are a parent for whom finding your baby's name is simply a case of seeing it written down then you'll love the dozens of lists we've included, highlighting the popular, the classic and the downright weird names children have been given over the years.

The average length of a baby name is six letters.

This book is broken into two sections: the first deals with how to figure out what to name your child through a series of questions and suggestions, and the second gives you a meaning for each name you're considering using. There's no right or wrong way to use this book, just as there's no right or wrong way to make your baby-naming decision, so dip in, find some names you like and use the suggestions we've given you to work out if one of them is a winner!

part one

Naming
Your Baby

1

What was hot in 2009?

> ❝Always end the name of your child with a vowel, so that when you yell the name will carry.❞
>
> Bill Crosby

The rise of quirky names

In 2008 and 2009 an interesting phenomenon took place: only 50% of babies born in the UK had their names represented in the Top 50 of recorded births. The remaining 50% all had such unique and diverse names that they did not get placed high enough in the charts to be listed. Although this has been the first time such a large number of names have not been represented, it has been a growing trend since the early 1980s. One possible explanation for this is that those children born since the early 1980s are now themselves having children. It seems likely that a parent with a slightly unusual name will feel more confident about giving their offspring a unique name if they have enjoyed their own growing up.

Some of Britain's quirky baby names included IKEA for a girl, Moet (after the champagne), Finchley (North London) and Ely (the cathedral city in Cambridgeshire) for boys.

2009 top 10 baby boy names

1. Jack
2. Oliver
3. Charlie
4. Alfie
5. Harry
6. Thomas
7. James
8. Joshua
9. William
10. Daniel

2009 top 10 baby girl names

1. Ruby
2. Olivia
3. Jessica
4. Grace
5. Sophie
6. Emily
7. Chloe
8. Lily
9. Amelia
10. Evie

Traditional names make a comeback

2009 also saw a continuation of the revival of previously outdated names. Names such as Alfie, Harry, Amelia and Ruby had dropped out of mainstream use by the 1960s and become vastly unpopular, but in the last five years names ending in –ie and –y have started to see a resurgence. 2009 was no different, with the Top 10 in both Boys and Girls names remaining largely unchanged. Other old-fashioned names, such as Ava, Dorothy and Noah have climbed the popularity ranks, joining such stalwarts as Emily, Jessica, Samuel and Matthew.

Incredibly, Jack has remained the top choice for parents of newborn baby boys 15 years in a row.

2009 popular boy name newcomers

- Ajay
- Alfie
- Danny
- Dawood
- Fergus
- Jayden
- Joseph
- Kian
- Lou
- Lui

2009 popular girl name newcomers

- Aizah
- Anastasia
- Daphne
- Denisa
- Hawa
- Iona
- Isabella
- Lacey
- Sarha
- Tira

For all the names coming into fashion, there are inevitably names that have slipped off the popular names list in the past years. This doesn't mean there isn't a perfect name for your baby in these lists too...

Girl names going out of fashion

- Alicia
- Demi
- Harriet
- Madeleine
- Shannon
- Francesca
- Maria
- Rose
- Sara

Boy names going out of fashion

- Billy
- Edward
- Elliot
- Finlay
- Kai
- Leo
- Oscar
- Reece/Rhys
- Reuben
- Toby

2

What does 2010 hold for baby names?

Will these trends continue?

Looking forward to 2010, the trend for choosing old-fashioned or unique names for babies seems set to continue. The Top 10 names will probably go largely unchanged for both boys and girls, but there may be a rise in the percentage of unique names not to make the Top 50.

Paradoxically, there may also be a backlash against very popular names, as parents opt to not give their child the same name as four or five of their potential school friends.

As parents grow more globally aware and the demographics of the UK change we may see more culturally and ethnically diverse names appearing in these lists, such as Ahmed, Aisha, Fatima and Mohammed.

Parents may also start looking further back into their family trees for inspiration, giving rise to many more African (Iman, Kwame), Asian (Mali, Thao) and Middle English names (Avery, Tate).

Predicted 2010 top 10 boy names

1. Jack
2. Oliver
3. Thomas
4. Charlie
5. Harry
6. Alfie
7. Joshua
8. Daniel
9. William
10. Mohammed

Predicted 2010 top 10 girl names

1. Ruby
2. Grace
3. Lily
4. Ella
5. Olivia
6. Emily
7. Amelia
8. Sophie
9. Chloe
10. Mia

2010 events

Other influences on the names parents choose in 2010 will come from the worlds of celebrity, politics and sport.

The name Theo, for example, saw an astonishing rise in popularity in recent years after the arrival of the teenage footballer Theo Walcott to the sporting world, jumping from rank number 70 in 2007 to the mid-50s in 2009. The 2010 FIFA World Cup, held in South Africa, may continue this love of Theo and possibly introduce some new popular names too, such as Darren (Bent), Jermain (Defoe), Shaun (Wright-Phillips) and Ashley (Young or Cole).

Competitors at the 2010 Vancouver Winter Olympics and Paralympics may also see their names appear on birth certificates the world over if any stars are made, suggesting a recurrence of the increase in children named Jane and Christopher after ice dancing stars Jane Torvill and Christopher Dean shot to sporting stardom in 1984.

The inauguration of US President Barack Obama in 2009 may continue to affect the popularity of the name Barack, and his wife's name Michelle. In 2007, the USA's Social Security Administration did not have the name Barack listed anywhere in its Top 100 most common baby names, but it is predicted to enter the Boys' list for the first time ever at the end of 2009.

The speculated engagement and then marriage of Prince William to Kate Middleton are sure to affect the status of the names William and Kate – if he gets a move on and pops the question.

With a national election imminent and the chance for a new Prime Minister to take office, 2010 may see a rise in the number of babies called David (Cameron) or Nick (Clegg), although having a new Prime Minister does not always dictate an increase in babies born with the same name: the name Gordon has yet to push its way back into the UK's Top 100 since Gordon Brown took office in 2007. Anthony also failed to remain popular during Tony Blair's time as PM; it was last seen in position number 98 in 2003 but has since dropped off the charts completely.

Also held in 2010 is the USA is the census, the results of which might determine the choices parents make for their baby names. Although US data does not always correspond to UK data, the statistics will be of definite interest to name historians on both sides of the pond, particularly those awaiting the 2011 UK census.

The cult of celebrity

As always, the world of celebrities will continue to dominate choices made by parents, for better or worse.

Celebrities expecting babies in late 2009 and 2010 include Angelina Jolie and Brad Pitt, and Sarah Michelle Gellar and Freddie Prinze Jr. If the choices of names these celebrities make are particularly noteworthy, they may well influence the choices made by the general population. The name Honor, for example, improved in popularity after the birth of Jessica Alba's baby girl in 2008, as well as the name Ava, which has even jumped in popularity with celebrities themselves. Reese Witherspoon has been given credit for this surge: after naming her daughter Ava in 1999, after actress Ava Gardner, the name jumped from rank number 259 to number 9 in 2005 and has stayed in the top five ever since.

In fact, after Britney Spears named her second son Jayden James in 2006, the name became the second most popular name for baby boys in New York City. Likewise, bad choices of names leave potential parents sniggering rather than considering, such as with the case of Bronx Mowgli, Ashlee Simpson's son or Princess Tiaamii, Jordan and Peter Andre's daughter.

Celebrity baby girls of 2009

Jennifer Garner and Ben Affleck:	Seraphina Rose Elizabeth (January 2009)
Gary Barlow and wife Dawn:	Daisy (January 2009)
Gareth Gates and wife Suzanne:	Missy (April 2009)
Jamie Oliver and wife Jools:	Petal Blossom Rainbow (April 2009)
Tess Daly and Vernon Kay:	Amber (June 2009)
Sarah Jessica Parker and husband Matthew Broderick:	Marion Loretta Elwell and Tabitha Hodge (July 2009)

Celebrity baby boys of 2009

Bear Grylls and wife Shara:	Huckleberry Edward Jocelyn (January 2009)
Charlotte Church and Gavin Henson:	Dexter Lloyd (January 2009)
Chris Evans and wife Tash:	Noah (February 2009)
Tiger Woods and wife Elin:	Charlie Axel (February 2009)
Sophie Ellis-Bextor and husband Richard:	Kit Valentine (February 2009)
Nick Clegg and wife Miriam:	Miguel (February 2009)
Parminder Nagra and partner James Stenson:	Kai David Singh (May 2009)
Robby Keane and wife Claudine:	Robert Ronan (May 2009)
Holly Willoughby and husband Dan:	Harry James (May 2009)
Tobey Maguire and wife Jennifer:	Otis Tobias (May 2009)
Lance Armstrong and Anna Hansen:	Max (June 2009)

Daft celebrity baby names of recent years

- Apple (Gwyneth Paltrow and Chris Martin)
- Blue Angel (U2's The Edge and Aislinn O'Sullivan)
- Bluebell Madonna (Geri Halliwell)
- Bronx Mowgli (Ashlee Simpson and Pete Wentz)
- Brooklyn (David and Victoria Beckham – also parents to Romeo and Cruz)
- Ikhyd (M.I.A. and Benjamin Brewer)
- Kal-El Coppola (Nicholas Cage – Kal-El is Superman's original birth name)
- Luna Coco Patricia (Frank Lampard and Elen Rive)
- Petal Blossom Rainbow (Jools and Jamie Oliver – also parents to Daisy Boo and Poppy Honey)
- Princess Tiaamii (Jordan and Peter Andre)
- Shiloh Nouvel (Brad Pitt and Angelina Jolie)
- Sunday Rose (Nicole Kidman and Keith Urban)
- Suri (Tom Cruise and Katie Holmes)
- Zuma Nesta Rock (Gwen Stefani and Gavin Rossdale)

Tom Cruise and Katie Holmes learnt a lesson about the woes of celebrity naming, when they found out their daughter Suris name meant 'from Syria' and not 'princess' in Hebrew, as they'd thought.

Expected celebrity babies

Nicole Ritchie and Joel Madden:	(August 2009)
Mel Gibson and girlfriend Oksana:	(Autumn 2009)
Sarah Michelle Gellar and Freddie Prinze Jr:	(Autumn 2009)
Jennifer Hudson and fiancé David:	(Autumn 2009)
Heidi Klum and Seal:	(Autumn 2009)
Coleen and Wayne Rooney:	(October 2009)
Gisele Bundchen and Tom Brady:	(December 2009)
Ben Fogle and wife Marina:	(December 2009)
Matthew McConaughey and girlfriend Camila Alves:	(Winter 2009)
Zoe Ball and Norman Cook:	(Winter 2009)

Significant dates in 2010

Significant anniversaries can potentially influence baby names.

In 2010 this includes the 90th anniversary of the first published Mickey Mouse cartoon, the 75th anniversary of the birth of Elvis Presley and the flight of the first woman, Amelia Earhart, to cross the Pacific Ocean solo.

Older anniversaries include the 200th year since the birth of composer Frédéric Chopin, the 100th year since the birth of Mother Teresa and the 100th celebration of the Alfa Romeo car brand.

Don't be surprised, therefore, if the names Mickey, Elvis, Amelia, Frederic, Teresa and Romeo all jump in popularity. The very fact these names will be bandied around by the media will mean parents will start to consider them as potential candidates, even if they would never have considered them previously.

2010 anniversary names

- Amelia
- Dorothea
- Elvis
- Frederic
- Henri
- Jacques
- Mickey
- Romeo
- Sandro
- Teresa

3

How to choose a name

Top tips on choosing a name

Fall in love with the name(s) you've chosen

If you plough through more than 200 pages of names in this book and none of them jump off the page at you, then you probably haven't found the right one yet. Likewise, if a relative, friend, or even your spouse suggests a name and you wrinkle your nose up every time you hear it, it's also not the name for your baby.

You will want to pick a name that you can shout with confidence across the school playground, or hear with pride when your child graduates from university. Pick a name which makes you smile because if you love it, hopefully they will too.

Don't listen to other people

Sometimes, grandparents and friends will offer 'advice' to you during this time which may not always be welcome. This is worth bearing in mind if you've fallen in love with a name and it's either slightly unusual or doesn't follow the set pattern your partner's family have used for the last 50 years. Sharing your choice of name with other people can lead them to criticise it, which you'd probably rather not hear if you've got your heart set on it. Also, if you're bucking tradition and don't plan on calling your newborn after their great-great-great-grandfather, keeping it a secret until after the birth and registration can work to your advantage. Trust your own instincts and remember: no-one will really care once they see your baby. Its name will simply be its name.

Unisex names

- Alex
- Dana
- Darryl/Daryl
- Frances/Francis
- Jude

- Lesley/Leslie
- Noel
- Robin
- Sidney/Sydney
- Teri/Terry

Research

You've already started the process of researching which name to pick simply by buying this book, but there are ways to expand the process if you wish to. The internet can be a fantastic way to look up meanings in more depth, or to find out if your baby's name is becoming more or less popular through the years. This is particularly useful if you want to avoid a situation where your daughter has the same name as three other children in her class, or if you don't want your son to be teased because his name sounds rude in another language. Other ways to do research include making lists of names you hear during the run-up to the birth, going back into history to find names of great cultural importance, or finding a meaning you like and linking a name to it. The name Helen, for example, means 'light', but there are a great many variations of it, including Aileen, Eleanor, Helena and Lena. Therefore, if you like the idea of naming your daughter 'light' but aren't keen on Helen, researching other variations might just lead you to the perfect one.

Find a name with meaning

When my parents discovered they were expecting a baby, they sought out possibilities that *meant* something. Both interested in history, they eventually settled on naming their three daughters after queens of England (Alexandra, Eleanor and Victoria) hoping to fill their children's souls with a sense of pride and importance. It worked, because throughout our lives we have all felt a duty to do our names justice in the modern world. Having a name which has a back story helps your child understand their significance in the world, so whether you name them after a religious saint or prophet, an important political figure or a hero in a Greek tragedy, ensure they know where their name came from. They may just be inspired to be as great as their namesake.

Have fun

Picking out names should be a fun process. Laughing at the ones you'd never dream of choosing can really help you narrow it down to the ones you would. You can also experiment with different spellings, pronunciations or variations of names you like, or go to places where you might feel inspired.

Some of the best names come from the worlds of nature and literature, so why not go down to your local garden centre or library and have fun with the classic, cute and downright silly words you find there?

Expand your mind

Don't rule out the weird ones just yet! As a teenager I went to school with a girl named Siam. Her parents had conceived her on a honeymoon trip to Thailand and given her the country's old name as a result. She loved growing up and having an unusual name, as I'm sure Brooklyn Beckham (Posh and Becks's son) and Bronx Wentz (Ashley Simpson and Pete Wentz's son) do too. Also, don't be afraid to play around with spellings and pronunciations, even if the results are a little less than conformist. The name Madison, for example, could be spelt Maddison, Madyson, Maddiesun or even Maddeesunn if you so choose, although you might want to be careful you don't saddle your child with an impossible name to spell, pronounce *and* fit onto a passport application form.

The shortest baby names are only two letters long (Al, Ed, Jo and Ty), but the longest could be any length imaginable. Popular 11-letter-long names include Bartholomew, Christopher, Constantine and Maximillian.

Try it out

While you're pregnant, talk to your baby and address it using a variety of your favourite names to see if it responds. There are numerous stories of names being chosen because the baby kicked when it was called Charlie or Aisha, but was suspiciously silent when it was called Dexter or Mildred, so see if it has a preference! You can also try writing names down and sticking them to your fridge, or saying one out loud enough times to see if you ever get sick of it. That name you picked out when you were eight and always said you'd name your first child, for example, might not sound so appropriate now you're an adult and have to name a human being for real.

What if you can't agree?

This is probably the trickiest problem in the baby-naming process to solve. It's wise to research a number of names you and your partner are both interested in and make a point of discussing your reasons for liking or disliking them long before the baby is due to be born.

The labour and delivery room is probably not the best time to argue about names as you'll both be tired, emotional and at least one of you will be in pain.

Avoid sticking to your guns on a name one of you really isn't happy with because it might lead to resentment down the line, with your baby caught in the middle. You could try compromising and picking two middle names so you both have a name in there you love, or you could each have five names you're allowed to 'veto' but no more. You could also try making contractions out of names you both like, such as Anna and Lisa (Annalisa) or James and Hayden (Jayden). Whichever way you go about it, it is important that you both eventually agree on the name you are giving your baby, even if it means losing out on that one you've had your heart set on for a while.

Popular girls' names from the past

- Agatha
- Bertha
- Clara
- Edith
- Gladys
- Mabel
- Pearl
- Theodora
- Wilhelmina
- Winifred

Popular boys' names from the past

- Abraham
- Arthur
- Edmund
- Emmett
- Franklin
- Gilbert
- Jasper
- Neville
- Percival
- Vincent

Things to consider when naming

Thinking to the future

❝ No, Groucho is not my real name. I'm breaking it in for a friend. ❞

Groucho Marx

One important aspect of naming your child is thinking ahead to their future. Will the name you've chosen stand the test of time? Will names popular in 2010 remain popular in 2035? Will they be able to confidently enter a room and give a crucial business presentation with an awkward or unpronounceable name? Will they be able to hand their business card over to a potential client without that client looking bemused every time? Even on a smaller scale, can they survive the potential minefields of primary and secondary school with a name that could be easily shortened to something embarrassing?

The first time your child encounters problems with their name will probably be before they're even born, or at least within the first few months. Many older siblings find new names hard to remember or pronounce and your baby could end up with a nickname before you know it. As an infant myself I was referred to as 'Baby Turner' by my older sister for the first few weeks, followed by 'Nell' once she realised I had a real name but couldn't say it properly. 'Nell' stuck from that moment on, and my family still finds it difficult to call me by my full name when I visit them, despite my many protestations.

If your baby has an older sibling, try talking to them about their new brother or sister using the name you've chosen so you can discover how their imagination might choose to interpret it.

If they're an older child you might even want to include them in the naming process from the start, if for no other reason than they mention a friend at school who gets teased for having an unfortunate nickname derived from the name you've chosen.

Banned names

The following names were all banned by registration officials in New Zealand:

- Cinderella Beauty Blossom
- Fat Boy
- Fish and Chips (twins)
- Keenan Got Lucy
- O.crnia
- Sex Fruit
- Stallion
- Talula Does The Hula From Hawaii
- Twisty Poi
- Yeah Detroit

New Zealand law prevents parents from giving their children names which would cause offence or are more than 100 characters long.

Allowed names

These names, however, were all permitted by the same officials:

- All Blacks
- Benson and Hedges (twins)
- Ford Mustang
- Kaos
- Masport and Mower (twins)
- Midnight Chardonnay
- Number 16 Bus Shelter
- Spiral Cicada
- Superman (changed from 4real)
- Violence

Nicknames are an unavoidable part of the history of names. Even seemingly simple names which do not lend themselves to being shortened can be subject to it: Prince Harry's real name, for example, is actually Henry, but he has been referred to as Harry since birth.

Nicknames can range from the common – Mike from Michael, Sam from Samantha – to the trendy, funny or downright insulting. My husband's brother was known as 'JoBi Wan Kenobi' from a very young age thanks to being given the name Joseph and I've lost count of the number of Richards who refuse to be called 'Dick' or the Francescas who prefer 'Fran' over 'Fanny'.

With all this said however, it is perfectly possible to choose a name which you know has an unfortunate nickname associated with it but for it to not bother you. If you don't encourage the use of nicknames when your child is young, chances are one won't stick when they're older either. I, for example, don't tell anyone I meet as an adult that I was known as Nell for the better half of my childhood, so no-one calls me that now.

Another way to avoid embarrassing nicknames is to select one for your child that you actually like so that others don't even get a mention. Call your daughter Elizabeth by Liz, Lizzie or Libby if you don't like Betty or Beth, and no-one will even consider the alternatives.

You can pre-empt problem nicknames to some extent by saying the name you've chosen out loud and trying to find rhymes for it. This is a clever way to avoid playground chants and nursery rhyme-type insults, such as Andy Pandy or Looby Lou. It's a sad truth though that children will rhyme anything with anything else if they can, so while you might wish to take playground chants into account during your naming process, don't be too concerned about them. Most children are subjected to it at some point and emerge unscathed.

A Chinese couple were prevented from naming their child '@' in 2007, despite their reasoning that it was simply a modern choice of name in this technological age.

One final consideration about your child's future you might want to think about is how your child will cope with that name as an adult. While this seems a very long way off now, it is important. Introducing themselves as Professor Xavier to a group of university deans might raise a few smirks among knowing *X-Men* fans, as would any unusual or trendy 2010 name which has lost its shine by 2035. Would you want to try catching criminals as Police Officer Apple Blossom or have other politicians take you seriously with a name like MP Lil' Kim Scarlett? You don't want to give your child a name which they just cannot live with for the rest of their lives, so make your choice based on what's appropriate for a child as well as an adult. To make this easier you might want to choose a longer name which can be shortened or extended as your child desires.

Initials

What surname will your baby have? Does its first letter lend itself easily to amusing acronyms already, and would choosing certain forenames only exacerbate the problem? If your child will inherit a double-barrelled surname this becomes a bigger consideration still, as there are more amusing four letter words than there are three. My brother-in-law was going to be called Andrew Steven Schmitt before he was born, until his parents realised at the last minute what his initials would spell...

It's worth taking the time to think about acronyms of initials in the real world too, such as how credit cards display names or seeing your child's name written out on a form.

Nobody should have to go through life known as Earl E. Bird, I. P. Freely or S. Lugg because their parents didn't think that far ahead. For a wonderful selection of these types of names, tune in to *The Simpsons* and observe Bart's prank phone calls to Moe's Tavern.

Amusing acronyms of real people

- David Vernon Durante – DVD
- George Barry Holmes – GBH
- Jake Clive Baxter – JCB
- James John Brookes – JJB (the sportswear shop)
- Jennifer Paige Garrett – JPG
- Neil Christopher Parker – NCP (the car park)
- Patricia Mary Simpson – PMS
- Samuel Alan Spencer – SAS
- Victoria Helen Smith – VHS

Across the UK, there are also people whose initials spell out three letter words – from RAT and FAG to FAB or POP (some are better than others so do check!).

Amusing initials

- Earl E Bird
- Kay F Cee
- I P Freely
- Al E Gador
- Angie O Graham

- S Lugg
- Warren T
- I C Blood
- H I Vee
- Gene E Yuss

Your surname

Connected to your child's potential new initials is their new surname. Whether they are receiving their name from their mother, father or a hyphenated combination of both, matching an appropriate first name to their surname is an important undertaking. Try to avoid forenames which might lead to unfortunate phrases when combined with certain surnames to prevent a lifetime of embarrassment for your baby.

The best way to work out if this might happen is to write down all the names you like alongside your child's last name and have someone else read them out loud. This second pair of eyes and ears might just spot something you didn't.

Unfortunate forename/surname combinations

- Anna Sasin
- Barb Dwyer
- Barry Cade
- Ben Dover
- Duane Pipe
- Grace Land
- Harry Rump
- Hazel Nutt
- Isabella Horn

- Jenny Taylor
- Justin Time
- Mary Christmas
- Oliver Sutton
- Paige Turner
- Russell Sprout
- Stan Still
- Teresa Green

There is also the danger of your child being subjected to having a spoonerism made out of their name, where the first letters or syllables get swapped around to form new words. An unfortunate and recent example of this would be Angelina Jolie and Brad Pitt's daughter Shiloh, whom they named Shiloh Jolie-Pitt to avoid the inevitable Shiloh Pitt spoonerism. Try to avoid making the same mistake!

French law prohibits all names other than those on an approved list.

Famous name spoonerisms

- Mike Baker (bike maker)
- Shirley Bassey (burly chassis)
- Kelly Brook (belly crook)
- Gordon Brown (broaden gown)
- Liz Fraser (frizz laser)
- Clive James (jive claims)
- Gene Kelly (keen jelly)
- Jude Law (lewd jaw)
- Sarah Palin (para sailing)
- Shiloh Pitt (pile o' s***)

Quirky names and stereotypes

There are lots of disadvantages to having a quirky name, but there are plenty of advantages too. For one thing, your child's name will never be forgotten by other people, and if they do something influential with their life their name could become inspirational for other parents to name their children. On the other hand, a quirky name often requires a quirky personality. If you don't think your genes could stand up to a name like Satchel or Kerensa, perhaps it's time to think of one a little more run-of-the-mill.

A quirky name often says more about the parents than the child, whose own personalities may affect the personality of their child in a significant way. A conventional family which names their baby John will probably find he becomes a conventional child, whereas a quirky family which names their baby Zanzibar will also find he develops a quirky personality. The name itself is not the leading factor; it's the quirky or conventional behaviour encouraged by the parents who chose the name that is.

It is not true that babies are as influenced by their names as people believe. There is no scientific evidence to say that names dictate who we become, which means that you cannot give your child a perfect or imperfect name, whichever one you finally pick.

What is usually the case is that people make assumptions about a name and that person's personality lives up to or fails those expectations. A boy named William might be expected to be intelligent, whereas one named Attila will be viewed automatically as a bully. A girl named Norma might be told her name is too old for her and one named Honey might be told it's too young. None of these assumptions, however, will change the personality of your child one iota, so if you want to choose a quirky name for them feel free to do so.

The one area you may wish to pause and consider is that of fictional and cartoon characters. Your baby is highly likely to be exposed to cartoons before they start school, so they will have their name associated with whatever their peers have read or seen. A boy named Barney or Fred, for example, might be teased for having the same name as a giant purple dinosaur or a stone-age cartoon character. A girl named Ariel or Belle might be expected to behave like a little princess, while one named Dorothy might be constantly asked if she wants to go home…

While avoiding any kind of possible connection to a fictional character is nigh on impossible, you can help make things easier for your child by educating them about their namesake and encouraging them to read more about them. Stay up-to-date with new cartoons and children's characters in 2010 to prepare both yourself and your child for toddlerdom and childhood. That way they can be proud of their name and have ammunition if things get rough in the playground.

It works the other way round too...

Cartoon characters named after real people

- Yogi Bear (named after baseball player Yogi Berra)
- Alvin, Simon and Theodore Chipmunk (named after record executives)
- Garfield (named after creator Jim Davis's grandfather)
- Calvin and Hobbes (named after John Calvin [theologian] and Thomas Hobbes [philosopher])
- Rock Lee (from *Naruto*, named after Bruce Lee)
- Alexander Lemming (from *The Beano*, named after scientist Alexander Fleming)
- Jimmy Neutron (named after the scientist James Chadwick, whose nickname was Jimmy Neutron)
- Oscar (from *Cerebus*, named after writer Oscar Wilde)
- Homer, Marge, Lisa and Maggie Simpson (named after creator Matt Groening's family members)
- Teenage Mutant Ninja Turtles (all named after Renaissance painters: Raphael, Michelangelo, Donatello and Leonardo)

Using family names

Some families have a strong tradition of using names for babies that come from the family tree. There are instances where naming your son Augustine VIII is simply not an option; it's a rule. Another way families do this is to give children the name of their parent of the same sex and add 'Junior' (Jr) to the end. This could potentially create a problem if that child then decides to carry on the tradition and name their child after themselves – after all, who wants to be known as Frederick Jr Jr?

There are obviously pros and cons with using family names:

Pros

- Your child will feel part of a strong tradition, which will create a sense of security for them and help make them feel a complete member of the family.

- If you're having a problem selecting a name you and your partner both agree on, this is a very simple solution and will make your new child's family very happy.

Cons

- You might not actually like the name that's being passed down. Naming your child the 12th Thumbelina in a row might not actually hold the same attraction for you as for the generation before you.

- Another drawback could be if the cultural associations with that name have changed in your lifetime and it is no longer appropriate.

One way to navigate around choosing a family name is to compromise.

You could use the name as a middle name, or refer to your baby by a nickname instead. You could also suggest using a name from the other partner's family: if the name comes from your side, try finding one you like from the other side. If their argument is for tradition then this is astonishingly effective.

Popular family names from 1904

Boys
- Albert
- Arthur
- Charles
- Ernest
- Frederick
- George
- James
- John
- Thomas
- William

Girls
- Alice
- Annie
- Doris
- Dorothy
- Edith
- Elizabeth
- Elsie
- Florence
- Margaret
- Mary

Popular family names from 1954

Boys
- Alan
- Christopher
- David
- John
- Michael
- Paul
- Peter
- Richard
- Robert
- Stephen

Girls
- Anne
- Carol
- Christine
- Elizabeth
- Janet
- Linda
- Margaret
- Mary
- Patricia
- Susan

Popular family names from 2004

Boys
- Benjamin
- Daniel
- Jack
- James
- Joseph
- Joshua
- Oliver
- Samuel
- Thomas
- William

Girls
- Charlotte
- Chloe
- Ellie
- Emily
- Jessica
- Katie
- Lucy
- Megan
- Olivia
- Sophie

Whatever you decide about using family names, just remember that this is *your* baby. Just as your parents got to decide what they named you, you get to decide this. If family and friends are disappointed, don't be alarmed. Once the baby is here they will only see how much she has her grandmother's nose, or his grandfather's ears, and the name will become far less important.

Spellings and pronunciation

Once you've finally agreed upon a name, it's time to consider how you wish it to be spelt and pronounced. Some parents take great joy in experimenting with unusual variations of traditional names, while others prefer names to be instantly recognisable. The only advice here is to use caution in your experiments. There are many anecdotal tales of parents seeing or hearing pretty names in the hospital during delivery and choosing them for their children, only to find out later they were medical terms and therefore completely inappropriate as names. Even spelling or pronouncing them differently won't be of much use once they're old enough to know the meaning behind them.

Actual medical terms used as names

- Arsehole (pronounced ar-SHOL-ee)
- Chlamydia
- Eczema
- Female (pronounced fuh-MAH-lee)
- Latrine (pronounced lah-TREE-nee)
- Meconium
- Syphilis
- Testicles (pronounced TESS-tee-clees)
- Urine (pronounced yer-REE-nee)
- Vagina (pronounced vaj-EE-nah)

Obviously the examples above are a little extreme, but the choices you make regarding spelling and pronunciation are really important. Try to avoid making a common name too long or too unusual in its spelling as this will be the first thing your child learns how to write. They will also be subjected to constant corrections during their lifetime, as other people misspell or mispronounce their name in ever more frustrating patterns.

Make sure the name isn't so long that it won't fit on forms or name badges as they'll simply stop using it and take on a nickname instead.

Substituting the odd 'i' for a 'y' isn't too bad, but turning the name Jonathan into Jonnaythanne doesn't do anyone any favours.

Britain has seen an increase in 'text' language spellings

- An
- Camron
- Conna
- Ema
- Esta
- Flicity
- Helin
- Jaicub
- Jayk
- Lora
- Patryk
- Samiul
- Summa

Middle names

The use of middle names is generally acknowledged to be standard practice in the UK these days. In fact, it has become fairly uncommon to name a child *without* a middle name, although there are cultures where this is still the case. A middle name can have just as much of an impact as a forename so your choice for your own baby should be made as carefully as their first name.

You may have already decided what middle name to give your child due to tradition or culture, in which case the following advice may be moot. In Spanish cultures, for example, middle names are often the mother's surname or other name to promote that matriarchal lineage. Similarly, parents who do not share the same surname may choose to give their child one surname as a middle name and one as a last name so both parents are represented. Other traditions may use an old family name, passed down to each first-born son or daughter to encourage a sense of family pride and history. A decision about what middle name to pass on may have therefore already been made for you, even before your own birth.

If you are choosing a middle name there are some common trends in 2010 to help you narrow it down.

Opposite-length names

It has become very popular to give a child either a long forename and short middle name, or a short forename and long middle name. If this idea attracts you, consider using syllables to give you an idea of length and combinations.

- Generally, if the forename has only one or two syllables (Owen, Steven, Yasmin, Zoe) then the middle name can have two, three or even four syllables (Owen Henri, Steven Michael, Yasmin Samantha, Zoe Jessica).

- If the opposite is true and the forename is three or four syllables long (Anthony, Jennifer, Nicholas, Rosemary), the middle name may be better kept to only one or two syllables (Anthony Kevin, Jennifer Ruth, Nicholas John, Rosemary Dawn). Of course, this rule may need to be tailored to your child's last name as a very long or hyphenated surname may suit a different combination entirely.

Name from the family tree

Honouring your ancestors is another popular trend for 2010. Parents are frequently looking back to their own lineage for interesting, unusual or influential names.

- If you know you or your partner is related to Charles Darwin, you might choose Charles or even Darwin as a middle name for your son, or if your great-great-grandmother had a particularly unusual name and worked in the Suffragette movement, you could choose her name for your daughter's middle name.

- If a relative passed away recently you could choose their name as a way of honouring their memory, or you could even choose it while they're still alive to make them proud.

- It is becoming more and more common to give a parent's first name as a middle name to newborns.

Unusual names

Along with a wider variety of first names in recent years (Ruby, Amelia and Mia have all climbed the Top 20 charts over the last five years, replacing the standard Emily, Chloe and Megan), parents are choosing more unusual middle names too. This would make sense, as a child named Bronte or Keilyn probably needs a fairly uncommon middle name to balance it out.

Alternatively, as middle names are far less frequently used, this is an opportunity for parents to have an unusual name included that they wouldn't perhaps use otherwise. If their child grows up not to like it they have the option of only using their initial, or simply dropping it from daily use altogether.

Common names

As a last resort, if you find you are struggling to pick a middle name you could always pick a traditionally used one. For girls, Anne, Marie, May and Rose have all been strikingly popular in 2009 and 2010 and the same is true for Andrew, David, James and Thomas for boys.

Popular middle names in 2010

Boys

- Adam
- Alexander
- Andrew
- David
- James
- Joseph
- Lee
- Michael
- Steven
- Thomas

Girls

- Anne
- Elise
- Elizabeth
- Grace
- Louise
- Marie
- May
- Nicole
- Rose
- Ruth

As with first names, middle names can have hilarious consequences if not thought about carefully. It's worth writing down your favourite combinations and saying them out loud to make sure you're not making one of these mistakes:

Amusing middle name combinations

- Blanche Kerr Tane (blanche curtain)
- Claire May Dye (Claire may die)
- Harry Armand Bach (hairy arm and back)
- Justin Miles North (just ten miles north)
- Laura Lynne Hardy (Laurel and Hardy)
- Liz May Read (Liz may read)
- Mary Annette Woodin (marionette wooden)
- Norma Leigh Lucid (normally lucid)
- May Ann Naze (mayonnaise)
- Sam Ann Fisher (salmon fisher)

Of course, you don't have to narrow down middle name choices to just one. It is becoming more and more common to have several middle names, particularly if parents like more than one or want to include a family name as well. Be careful not to have too many though, as this makes life very difficult when filling out official forms or enrolling your child in school. Most institutions only recognise one middle name, and some only recognise a middle initial.

The Glastonbury teenager named **Captain Fantastic Faster Than Superman Spiderman Batman Wolverine Hulk And The Flash Combined**, changed his name from George Garratt in 2008. He claims to have the longest name in the world. If he does then he replaces Texan woman **Rhoshandiatellyneshiaunneveshenk Koyaanisquatsiuth Williams**, whose 57-letter length name pales in comparison to Captain's 81.

One last thing to bear in mind when choosing a middle name is that many people actually choose to go by this name instead of their forename. Celebrities often do this so they can be identified separately to other people of the same name (Brad Pitt's real name is William Bradley Pitt, for example), but it is just as common for non-celebrities too. In fact, you probably know someone in your family or workplace that has always been known as Ed or Sam when their name is actually James Edward Jones or Felicity Samantha Taylor. You might even choose to do this with your own child, particularly if you're using a family name and adding Jr to the title. It might be easier to call James Jones Jr Ed, if only to make it clear who you're telling off at the dinner table!

Celebrities who go by middle names

- Antonio Banderas (Jose Antonio Dominguez Banderas)
- Bob Marley (Nesta Robert Marley)
- Dakota Fanning (Hannah Dakota Fanning)
- Will Ferrell (John William Ferrell)
- Kelsey Grammer (Allen Kelsey Grammer)
- Ashton Kutcher (Christopher Ashton Kutcher)
- Hugh Laurie (James Hugh Calum Laurie)
- Evangeline Lilly (Nicole Evangeline Lilly)
- Brad Pitt (William Bradley Pitt)
- Brooke Shields (Christa Brooke Camille Shields)
- Reese Witherspoon (Laura Jean Reese Witherspoon)

The science of baby naming

❝From our ancestors come our names, but from our virtues our honours. ❞

Proverb

Whether you agree with it or not, there is a certain science to naming babies. Even at the very basic level of choosing a name you like the sound of, the science is there.

Some experts have noted that parents who choose inspirational names for their offspring (Destiny, Serenity, Unique) or names of products they aspire to own (Armani, Jaguar, Mercedes) are projecting a future onto their child for them to aspire to. After all, the idea of a Mercedes working at a local fast-food restaurant isn't nearly as attractive as one who works as a lawyer or artist.

Inspirational names

- Destiny
- Happy
- Heaven
- Hope
- Innocence

- Joy
- Peace
- Serenity
- Unique
- Unity

Future aspirations names

- Armani
- Aston
- Bugatti
- Chanel
- Dolce

- Ferrari
- Jaguar
- Mercedes
- Porsche
- Prada

Oxbridge names

- Alcott
- Arthur
- Beatrice
- Caroline
- Charles

- Graydon
- Katherine
- Martha
- Robert
- Victoria

Popular names of English and Scottish kings and consorts

- Alexander
- Charles
- Edward
- George
- Henry

- James
- Richard
- Robert
- Stephen
- William

Popular names of US presidents

- Abraham (Lincoln)
- Andrew (Jackson, Johnson)
- Barack (Obama)
- Franklin (Pierce, Roosevelt)
- George (Washington, H. Bush, W. Bush)
- James (Madison, Monroe, Knox Polk, Buchanan, Garfield, Carter)
- John (Adams, Quincy Adams, Tyler, Kennedy)
- Richard (Nixon)
- Ronald (Reagan)
- William (Henry Harrison, McKinley, Howard Taft, Clinton)

Popular names of English and Scottish queens and consorts

- Anna
- Anne
- Catherine
- Eleanor
- Elizabeth

- Mairi
- Margaret
- Mary
- Matilda
- Victoria

Popular names of UK prime ministers

- Anthony (Eden, Blair)
- Arthur (Wellesley, Balfour, Neville Chamberlain)
- Charles (Wentworth, Grey)
- George (Grenville, Canning, Gordon)
- Gordon (Brown)
- Harold (Macmillan, Wilson)
- Henry (Pelham, Fitzroy, Addington, Temple, Campbell-Bannerman, Asquith)
- James (Balfour, MacDonald, Wilson)
- John (Stuart, Russell, Major)
- Robert (Walpole, Jenkinson, Peel, Gascoyne-Cecil)
- Spencer (Crompton, Perceval)
- William (Cavendish, Pitt (Elder), Fitzmaurice, Cavendish-Bentinck, Pitt (Younger), Wyndham, Lamb, Gladstone)

If you're interested in comic books and superheroes, why not consider using them for inspiration? Nicholas Cage named his second son Kal-El, which is Superman's real name, and a New Zealand couple even went as far as to actually name their baby boy Superman after 4real was rejected by authorities.

While parents are often cautioned or even discouraged from picking wild and crazy names for their babies (think about Petal Blossom Rainbow, Jamie Oliver's third daughter) there isn't actually any scientific evidence to suggest that children are hindered in any way by them. There seems to be more evidence to suggest that the stories behind names are more important.

Children who are told they have inherited an ancestor's name or that of an influential character from history seem to be more driven and focused than children who are told disappointingly, 'We just liked the sound of it'. As a parent, therefore, it seems it's okay to pick an unusual name if you have the story or anecdotal evidence to back it up.

Another thing to consider about the science of baby naming is how your child's name will be perceived by the outside world. Typically, judgements are passed on names before a person is met, such as at job interviews or in school. This does have the potential to hold back your child, although there is conflicting evidence to say that once someone is met in person, assumptions and stereotypes are wiped away.

Personality and character have a far greater influence than name alone and after a while, a name becomes just a name.

It is wise to be cautious though, particularly if the name you're considering is extremely controversial. In the United States in December 2008 there was a case of a supermarket bakery refusing to ice the words 'Happy Birthday, Adolf Hitler' onto a three year old's birthday cake, despite never having met the child it was intended for. The parents were able to eventually fulfil the order at another shop, but as a result of the publicity surrounding the event Social Services were called in to assess the child's home and Adolf, along with his siblings JoyceLynn Aryan Nation and Honszlynn Hinler Jeannie, were taken into care.

Controversial names adopted by real people

- Adolf Hitler
- Beelzebub
- Desdemona
- Hannibal Lecter
- Himmler
- Jezebel
- Lucifer
- Mussolini
- Stalin
- Voldemort

If your child will be given a name from an ethnic or cultural heritage, there is often a fear that this will potentially hold them back. Many children from a Chinese heritage, for example, choose to adopt a Western name while at school rather than have countless teachers and classmates mispronounce or make judgements about their name.

Another example would be strong Islamic names (think Ahmed, Mohammed or Neha), which given the current political climate, some children and teenagers fear could prevent them from being treated fairly at school or in their first job. This is not to say that these names should not be used, as it is the fault of prejudiced people passing judgements on your child's name rather than the fault of the name itself. In fact, the greater the diversity of names and cultures represented by them, the greater the chance of society's acceptance overall.

Names which mean 'clever'

- Abner
- Cassidy
- Haley
- Penelope
- Portia
- Shanahan
- Todd
- Ulysses
- Washington
- Wylie

Names which sound 'clever'

- Alastair
- Charles
- Christian
- Elizabeth
- Frances
- Gabriel
- Harriet
- Sophia
- Spencer
- William

4

Naming twins, triplets and more

If you have discovered you are expecting multiples, con-gratulations! Naming multiples needn't be any different to naming a single child... unless you want it to be. You could stick to the same process everyone else does, by picking an individual name for each individual child, or you could go with a theme. Try anagrams or names in reverse, or give each child the same initials. You could even do this if you're not expecting multiples, like the Duggar family of Arkansas, USA, who have given each of their 18 children the initial 'J'.

Twin anagram combinations

- Blake and Kaleb
- Dean and Aden
- Edna and Dena
- Ira and Ria
- Johan and Jonah
- Lisa and Ilsa
- Mary and Myra
- Moira and Mario
- Noel and Leon
- Reva and Vera

A palindrome name is a name which is spelt the same backwards and forwards, as with Bob, Elle, Eve and Hannah.

Twin names with the same meaning

- Bernard and Brian (strong)
- Daphne and Laura (laurel)
- Deborah and Melissa (bee)
- Dorcas and Tabitha (gazelle)
- Elijah and Joel (God)
- Eve and Zoe (life)
- Irene and Salome (peace)
- Lucius and Uri (light)
- Lucy and Helen (light)
- Sarah and Almira (princess)

Popular twin names in 2009

- Brandon and Brian
- Daniel and David
- Ella and Emma
- Faith and Hope
- Gabriella and Isabella
- Isaac and Isaiah
- Jacob and Joshua
- Madison and Morgan
- Matthew and Michael
- Taylor and Tyler

Of course, when all's said and done you can just stick to giving each child a name unique to them. For triplets, quads and more this is probably an easier choice than twisting your head around three names with the same meaning, or trying to create four anagrams you like for all of your babies. Some parents do like to use a theme though, such as matching initials or names that go down the alphabet (think Alastair, Benjamin, Christopher and David).

The likelihood of women conceiving multiples in the 21st century is on the rise, which experts have attributed to couples delaying having children until later in life (women over 30 are more likely to have multiples) and more couples having access to affordable fertility treatments (fertility drugs have a higher rate of multiple-birth pregnancies than normal). It's also becoming very common for celebrities to have multiple births these days, for exactly the same reasons as the rest of us. However, not all of them have stuck to a theme with names.

In fact, the most famous recent example of a mother with a multiple pregnancy chose eight different names for her octuplets, although they do all sound reasonably similar: Isaiah, Jeremiah, Jonah, Josiah, Maliah, McCai, Nariah and Noah. Nadya Suleman, also known as Octomom, delivered her eight babies in January 2009, expanding her brood to a total of 14 children.

Recent celebrity twin names

- Darby and Sullivan (Patrick Dempsey and Jillian Fink)
- Dexter and Frank (Elvis Costello and Diana Krall)
- Eden and Savannah (Marcia Cross and Tom Mahoney)
- Finlay and Harper (Lisa Marie Presley and Michael Lockwood)
- Hazel and Phinnaeus (Julia Roberts and Danny Moder)
- Jesse and Journey (Jenna Jameson and Tito Ortiz)
- Jett and Shannon (Pat Cash and Emily Bendit)
- Max and Bob (Charlie Sheen and Brooke Mueller)
- Max and Emme (Jennifer Lopez and Marc Anthony)
- Vivienne Marcheline and Knox Leon (Angelina Jolie and Brad Pitt)

Names for triplets

- Abel, Bela and Elba (anagrams)
- Aidan, Diana and Nadia (anagrams)
- April, May and June (months)
- Amber, Jade and Ruby (jewels)
- Amy, May and Mya (anagrams)
- Ava, Eva and Iva (similar)
- Daisy, Lily and Rose (flowers)
- Jay, Raven and Robin (birds)
- Leah, Lianne and Liam (similar)
- Olive, Violet and Sage (colours)

5

Registering a baby name

There are slightly different guidelines for registering births and names depending on where you live in the UK:

In England, Wales and Northern Ireland

A birth must be recorded within 42 days of delivery and if not done at the hospital it requires a visit to a register office.

- The birth certificate will be written in English if a child is born in England or Northern Ireland, and can be in both English and Welsh if they are born in Wales.

- If your baby is recorded at the hospital or in the same district as the birth itself then birth certificates are usually issued straightaway, but if you end up going to a different office the certificate may be sent to you after a few days. This is important when applying for Child Benefits or registering your baby with a doctor as you will need a copy of the short birth certificate to apply.

- If the parents of a newborn are married, either parent can register a birth. However, if the parents are not married there are several ways to ensure both names are put on the birth certificate, including both parents being physically present at the registration or one parent submitting a declaration form in lieu of their presence. If neither parent can be present then someone who was present at the birth or someone who is now responsible for the child can also carry out the duty.

- After the registration parents or those with parental responsibility also have the option of requesting a naming ceremony. These non-religious ceremonies are conducted by local authorities and can be a nice replacement for a baptism or christening as adults outside of the family can be nominated to act in secular roles similar to godparents. A birth certificate is also needed for this event to take place.

In Scotland

Births need to be registered within 21 days and registration can take place in any district. As well as either married parents being allowed to register the birth, relatives of those parent may also do the duty. The exception here is if the parents are not married. In this case the father may only register the birth if the mother is also present, a declaration form is submitted or a court agrees that he has parental responsibility just like any other adult. Parents of newborns in Scotland should take a card given to them at the hospital and a copy of their marriage certificate to the birth registration.

Useful websites:
Registering a birth in England and Wales: www.direct.gov.uk
Registering a birth in Northern Ireland: www.groni.gov.uk
Registering a birth in Scotland: www.gro-scotland.gov.uk

Making changes

If you decide at a later stage you want to change details on the birth certificate there are procedures in place to help, although it is often a time-consuming process.

- It is worth remembering that if the father's details were not recorded on the original certificate or if the natural parents have married since the registration, a new birth certificate will have to be generated. Both changes require filling out an application form, available on the websites listed above.

- If the forename you've chosen has been spelt incorrectly you can change the birth record providing you have other documentation to prove this is the case. A passport or baptismal certificate is sufficient as they will show the correct spelling or commonly used forename and should be presented to the register office where the initial application was made.

- If you wish to change the surname of your baby it is only possible in two cases: either the spelling is incorrect or the details of the parents are being changed (such as the inclusion of the father or the parents now being married). Again, evidence and form submissions are needed to make any changes and a fee is usually incurred if a new certificate is required.

Keep in mind how difficult it may be for you to change your child's birth certificate at a later stage if you are in any way unsure about the choice you're about to make. However, also remember that if something unexpected happens and you need to make the change, it is possible. There are stories of drunken fathers registering the birth of their child alone with a name not agreed upon by the mother, much to her horror. As Robert Eisenschmidt says, 'I have a friend, Bill Land, who named his daughter Alison Wanda Land. His wife changed the name on the birth certificate when she found out.' So it is possible, though obviously not preferred.

part two

Boys'
Names

Boys' names

Aaron

Hebrew, meaning 'mountain of strength'.

Abasi

Egyptian, meaning 'male'.

Abdiel

Biblical, meaning 'servant of God'.

Abdul

Arabic, meaning 'servant'. Often followed with a suffix indicating who Abdul is the servant of (eg Abdul-Basit, servant of the creator).

Abdullah

Arabic, meaning 'servant of God'.

Abe

Hebrew, from Abraham, meaning 'father'.

Abel

Hebrew, meaning 'breath' or 'breathing spirit'. Associated with the Biblical son of Adam and Eve who was killed by his brother Cain.

Abelard

German, meaning 'resolute'.

Aberforth

Gaelic, meaning 'mouth of the river Forth'. Name of Dumbledore's brother in the *Harry Potter* books.

A

Abhishek

Indian, meaning 'bath for a deity' or 'anointing'.

Abner

Biblical Hebrew, meaning 'father of light'.

Absalom
(alt. Absalon)

Hebrew, meaning 'father/ leader of peace'.

Acacio

Greek origin, meaning 'thorny tree'. Now widely used in Spain.

Ace

English, meaning 'number one' or 'the best'.

Achebe

Nigerian. Surname of famous writer Chinua Achebe.

Achilles

Greek. Mythological hero of Trojan war, whose heel was his only weak spot.

Achim

Hebrew, meaning 'God will establish' or Polish, meaning 'The Lord exalts'.

Ackerley

Old English, meaning 'oak meadow'. Often used as surname, many similarly spelt variants.

Adalberto

Germanic/Spanish, meaning 'nobly bright'.

Adam

Hebrew, meaning 'man' or 'earth'. First man to walk the earth, accompanied by Eve.

Adão

Variant of Adam, meaning 'earth'.

Addison

Old English, meaning 'son of Adam'. Also used as a female name in the USA.

Ade

African, meaning 'peak' or 'pinnacle'.

A

Adelard

Teutonic, meaning 'brave' or 'noble'.

Adelbert

Old German form of Albert.

Aden

Gaelic, meaning 'fire'.

Adetokunbo

Yoruba, meaning 'the crown came from over the sea'.

Adin

Hebrew, meaning 'slender' or 'voluptuous'. Also Swahili, meaning 'ornamental'.

Aditya

Sanskrit, meaning 'belonging to the sun'.

Adlai

Hebrew, meaning 'God is just', or sometimes 'ornamental'.

Adler

Old German, meaning 'eagle'.

Adley

English, meaning 'son of Adam'.

Admon

Hebrew origin, variant of Adam meaning 'earth'. Also the name of a red peony.

Adolph

Old German, meaning 'noble majestic wolf'. Popularity of the name plummeted after the Second World War, for obvious reasons.

Movie inspirations

Anakin (*Star Wars*)
Austin (*Austin Powers*)
Conan (*Conan the Barbarian*)
Dade (*Hackers*)
Inigo (*Princess Bride*)
Korben (*The Fifth Element*)
Marty (*Back to the Future*)
Otto (*A Fish Called Wanda*)
Renton (*Trainspotting*)
Wayne (*Wayne's World*)

Adonis

Phoenician, meaning 'Lord'.

Adrian

Latin origin, meaning 'from Hadria', a town in northern Italy.

Adriel

Biblical Hebrew, meaning 'of God's flock'.

Aeneas

Greek/Latin origin, meaning 'to praise'. Name of the hero who founded Rome in Virgil's *Aeneid*.

Aeson

Greek origin, father of Jason.

Afonso

Portuguese, meaning 'eager noble warrior'.

Agamemnon

Greek. Figure in mythology, commanded the Greeks at the siege of Troy.

Agathon

Greek, meaning 'good' or 'superior'.

Agustin

Latin/Spanish, meaning 'venerated'.

Ahab

Hebrew, meaning 'father's brother'. Pleasant way to address an uncle.

Ahijah

Biblical Hebrew, meaning 'brother of God' or 'friend of God'.

Ahmed

Arabic/Turkish, meaning 'worthy of praise'.

Aidan

Gaelic, meaning 'little fire'.

Aidric

Old English, meaning 'oaken'.

Airyck

Old Norse, from Eric, meaning 'eternal ruler'.

Ajani

African, meaning 'he fights for what he is'. Also Sanskrit, meaning 'of noble birth'.

Ajax

Greek, meaning 'mourner of the Earth'. Another Greek hero from the siege of Troy.

Ajay

Indian, meaning 'unconquerable'.

Ajit

Indian, meaning 'invincible'.

Akeem

Arabic, meaning 'wise or insightful'.

Akio

Japanese, meaning 'bright man'.

Akira

Japanese, meaning 'intelligent'.

Akiva

Hebrew, meaning 'to protect' or 'to shelter'.

Akon

American, made popular by the famous rapper charting in 2008/2009.

Aksel

Hebrew/Danish, meaning 'father of peace'.

Aladdin

Arabic, meaning 'servant of Allah'. Popular Disney character.

Alan

(alt.Allan, Allen, Allyn, Alun)

Gaelic, meaning 'rock'.

Alaric

Old German, meaning 'noble regal ruler'.

Alastair

(alt. Alasdair, Allister)

Greek/Gaelic, meaning 'defending men'.

Alban

Latin, meaning 'from Alba'. Also the Welsh and Scottish Gaelic word for 'Scotland'.

A

Alberic

Germanic, meaning 'Elfin king'.

Albert

Old German, meaning 'noble, bright, famous'.

Albin

Latin, meaning 'white'.

Albus

Latin, variant of Albin meaning 'white'. Also the Christian name of Albus Dumbledore, headmaster of Hogwarts School in the *Harry Potter* books.

Alcaeus

Greek, meaning 'strength'.

Alden

Old English, meaning 'old friend'.

Aldis

English, meaning 'from the old house'.

Aldo

Italian origin, meaning 'old' or 'elder'.

Aldric

English, meaning 'old King'.

Alec

(alt. Alek)

English, meaning 'defending men'.

Aled

Welsh, meaning 'child' or 'offspring'.

Alessio

Italian, meaning 'defender'.

Alexander

(alt. Alex)

Greek origin, meaning 'defending men'.

Alexei

Russian origin, meaning 'defender'.

Alfonso

Germanic/Spanish, meaning 'noble and prompt, ready to struggle'.

Alford

Old English, meaning 'old river/ ford'.

Alfred

(alt. Alf, Alfi)

English, meaning 'elf' or 'magical counsel'.

Algernon

French origin, meaning 'with a moustache'.

Ali

(alt. Allie)

Arabic, meaning 'noble, sublime'.

Allison

English, meaning 'noble'.

Alois

German, meaning 'famous warrior'.

Alok

Indian, meaning 'cry of triumph'.

Alon

Jewish, meaning 'oak tree'.

Alonso

(alt. Alonzo)

Germanic, meaning 'noble and ready'.

Aloysius

Italian saint's name, meaning 'fame and war'.

Alpha

First letter of the Greek alphabet.

Alphaeus

Hebrew origin, meaning 'changing'.

Alpin

Gaelic, meaning 'related to the Alps'.

Altair

Arabic, meaning 'flying' or 'bird'.

Alter

Yiddish, meaning 'old man'.

Alton

Old English, meaning 'old town'.

A

Alva
Latin, meaning 'white'.

Alvie
German, meaning 'army of elves'.

Alvin
English, meaning 'friend of elves'.

Alwyn
Welsh, meaning 'wise friend'. May also come from the River Alwen in Wales.

Amachi
African, meaning 'who knows what God has brought us through this child'.

Amadeus
Latin, meaning 'God's love'.

Amadi
African, meaning 'appeared destined to die at birth'.

Amado
Spanish, meaning 'God's love'.

Amador
Spanish, meaning 'one who loves'.

Amari
Hebrew, meaning 'given by God'.

Amarion
Arabic, meaning 'populous, flushing'.

Amasa
Hebrew, meaning 'burden'.

Ambrose
Greek, meaning 'undying, immortal'.

Americo
Germanic, meaning 'ever powerful in battle'.

Amias
Latin, meaning 'loved'.

Amir
Hebrew, meaning 'prince' or 'treetop'.

A

Amit

Hindu, meaning 'friend'.

Ammon

Egyptian, meaning 'the hidden one'.

Amory

German/English, meaning 'work' and 'power'.

Amos

Hebrew, meaning 'encumbered' or 'burdened'.

Anacletus

Latin, meaning 'called back' or 'invoked'.

Anakin

American, meaning 'warrior'. Made famous by Anakin Skywalker in the *Star Wars* films.

Ananias

Greek/Italian, meaning 'answered by the Lord'.

Anastasius

Latin, meaning 'resurrection'.

Anat

Jewish, meaning 'water spring'.

Anatole

Greek, meaning 'cynical but without malice'.

Anders

Greek, meaning 'lion man'.

Anderson

English, meaning 'male'.

Andrew
(alt. Andreas)

Greek, meaning 'man' or 'warrior'.

Androcles

Greek, meaning 'glory of a warrior'.

Angel

Greek, meaning 'messenger'.

Angus

Scottish, meaning 'one choice'.

Anil

Sanskrit, meaning 'air' or 'wind'.

A

Anselm

German, meaning 'helmet of God'.

Anson

English, meaning 'son of Agnes'.

Anthony

English, from the old Roman family name.

Antipas

Israeli, meaning 'for all or against all'.

Antwan

Old English, meaning 'flower'.

Apollo

Greek, meaning 'to destroy'. Greek god of the sun.

Apostolos

Greek, meaning 'apostle'.

Ara

Armenian. Ara was a legendary king.

Aragorn

Literary, used by Tolkien in *The Lord of the Rings* trilogy.

Aram

Biblical, meaning 'Royal Highness'.

Aramis

Latin, meaning 'swordsman'.

Arandu

Place in Pakistan, meaning 'little garden'.

Arcadio

Greek/Spanish, from a place in ancient Greece. The word 'Arcadia' (meaning paradise) comes from this.

Archibald
(alt.Archie)

Old German, meaning 'genuine/bold/brave'.

Ardell

Latin, meaning 'eager/burning with enthusiasm'.

Arden

Celtic, meaning 'high'.

A

Ares

Greek, meaning 'ruin'. Son of Zeus and Greek god of war.

Ari

Hebrew, meaning 'lion' or 'eagle'.

Arias

Germanic, meaning 'lion'.

Ariel

Hebrew, meaning 'lion of God'. One of the archangels, angel of healing and new beginnings.

Arild

Old Norse, meaning 'battle commander'.

Aris

Greek, meaning 'best figure'.

Ariston

Greek, meaning 'the best'.

Aristotle

Greek, meaning 'best'. Famous philosopher.

Arjun

Sanskrit, meaning 'white'.

Arkady

Greek, region of central Greece.

Arlan

Gaelic, meaning 'pledge' or 'oath'.

Arlie

Old English place name, meaning 'eagle wood'.

Arlis

Hebrew, meaning 'pledge'.

Arlo

Spanish, meaning 'barberry tree'.

Armand

Old German, meaning 'soldier'.

Armani

Same origin as Armand meaning 'soldier', nowadays closely associated with the Italian designer.

A

Arnaldo

Spanish, meaning 'eagle power'.

Arnav

Indian, meaning 'the sea'.

Arnold

Old German, meaning 'eagle ruler'.

Arrow

English, from the common word denoting weaponry.

Art

Irish, name of a warrior in Irish mythology, Art Oenfer (Art the Lonely).

Arthur

(alt. Artie, Artis)

Celtic, probably from 'artos', meaning 'bear'. Made famous by the tales of King Arthur and the Knights of the Round Table.

Arvel

From the Welsh 'Arwel', meaning 'wept over'.

Arvid

English, meaning 'eagle in the woods'.

Arvind

Indian, meaning 'red lotus'.

Arvo

Finnish, meaning 'value' or 'worth'.

Arwen

Welsh, meaning 'fair' or 'fine'.

Asa

Hebrew, meaning 'doctor' or 'healer'.

Asante

African, meaning 'thank you'.

Asher

Hebrew, meaning 'fortunate' or 'lucky'.

Ashley

Old English, meaning 'ash meadow'.

Ashok

Sanskrit, meaning 'not causing sorrow'.

A

Ashton

English, meaning 'settlement in the ash-tree grove'.

Aslan

Turkish, meaning 'lion'. Strongly associated with the lion from C S Lewis' *The Lion, The Witch, and The Wardrobe*.

Asriel

Biblical origin, meaning 'help of God'.

Astrophel

Latin, meaning 'star lover'.

Athanasios

Greek origin, meaning 'eternal life'.

Atílio

Portuguese, meaning 'father'.

Atlas

Greek, meaning 'to carry'. In Greek mythology Atlas was a Titan forced to carry the weight of the heavens.

Atlee

Hebrew, meaning 'God is just'.

Atticus

Latin, meaning 'from Athens'.

Literary names

Charlie (*Charlie and the Chocolate Factory*, Roald Dahl)
Christopher (*Now We Are Six*, A. A. Milne)
Darcy (*Pride and Prejudice*, Jane Austen)
Dorian (*The Picture of Dorian Gray*, Oscar Wilde)
Ishmael (*Moby-Dick*, Herman Melville)
James (*James Bond* series, Ian Fleming)
Oliver (*Oliver Twist*, Charles Dickens)
Lemuel (*Gulliver's Travels*, Jonathan Swift)
Regan (*King Lear*, William Shakespeare)
Tom (*Tom Jones*, Henry Fielding)

A

Auberon

Old German, meaning 'royal bear'.

Aubrey

Old German, meaning 'power'.

Auden

Old English, meaning 'old friend'.

Audie

Old English, meaning 'noble strength'.

Augustas

(alt. Augustus)

Latin, meaning 'venerated'.

Aurelien

French, meaning 'golden'.

Austin

Latin, meaning 'venerated'. Also city in the state of Texas in America.

Avi

Hebrew, meaning 'father of a multitude of nations'.

Awnan

Irish, meaning 'little Adam'.

Axel

Hebrew, meaning 'father is peace'. Made famous by Guns 'n' Roses front man Axl Rose.

Azarel

Hebrew, meaning 'helped by God'.

Azaryah

Hebrew, meaning 'helped by God'.

Azriel

Hebrew, meaning 'God is my help'.

Azuko

African, meaning 'past glory'.

B

Boys' names

Baden

German origin, meaning 'battle'.

Bailey

English, meaning 'bailiff'.

Baird

Scottish, meaning 'poet' or 'one who sings ballads'.

Bakari

Swahili, meaning 'hope' or 'promise'.

Baker

English, from the word baker.

Baldwin

Old French, meaning 'bold, brave friend'.

Balin

Old English. Balin was one of the knights of the Round Table.

Balthazar

Babylonian, meaning 'protect the King'.

Balvinder

Hindu, meaning 'merciful, compassionate'.

Bannon

Irish, descendant of O'Banain. Also a river in Wales.

B

Barack

African, meaning 'blessed'. Made popular by US President Barack Obama.

Barclay

Old English, meaning 'birch tree meadow'.

Barker

Old English, meaning 'shepherd'.

Barnaby
(alt. Barney)

Greek, meaning 'son of consolation'.

Barnard

English, meaning 'strong as a bear'.

Baron

Old English, meaning 'young warrior'.

Barrett

English, meaning 'strong as a bear'.

Barron

Old German, meaning 'old clearing'.

Barry

Irish Gaelic, meaning 'fair haired'. Also a town in South Wales, made popular by the BBC television series *Gavin and Stacey*.

Bart
(from Bartholomew)

Hebrew, meaning 'son of the farmer'. Made popular by the famous American TV character Bart Simpson.

Barton

Old English, meaning 'barley settlement'.

Baruch

Hebrew, meaning 'blessed'.

Bascom

Old English, meaning 'from Bascombe' (in Dorset).

Bashir

Arabic, meaning 'well-educated' and 'wise'.

B

Basil
Greek, meaning 'royal, kingly'.

Basim
Arabic, meaning 'smile'.

Bastien
Greek, meaning 'revered'.

Baxter
Old English, meaning 'baker'.

Bayard
French, meaning 'auburn haired'.

Bayo
Nigerian, meaning 'to find joy'.

Baz
Irish Gaelic, meaning 'fair-haired'.

Beau
French, meaning 'handsome'.

Beck
Old Norse, meaning 'stream'.

Beckett
Old English, meaning 'beehive' or 'bee cottage'. Associated with the Irish writer Samuel Beckett.

Beckham
English, meaning 'homestead by the stream'. Made famous by David and Victoria Beckham.

Béla
Hungarian, meaning 'within'.

Belarius
Shakespearean, meaning 'a banished lord'.

Biblical names

David
John
Joseph
Luke
Mark
Matthew
Michael
Paul
Peter
Simon

B

Benedict

Latin, meaning 'blessed'.

Benjamin

(alt. Ben)

Hebrew, meaning 'son of the south'.

Bennett

French/Latin vernacular form of Benedict, meaning 'blessed'.

Benoit

French form of Benedict, meaning 'blessed'.

Benson

English, meaning 'son of Ben'. Also linked to the village of Benson in Oxfordshire.

Bentley

Old English, meaning 'bent grass meadow'.

Benton

Old English, meaning 'town in the bent grass'.

Beriah

Biblical, meaning 'in fellowship' or 'in envy'.

Bernard

(alt. Bernie)

Germanic, meaning 'strong, brave bear'.

Berry

Old English, meaning 'berry'.

Bert

(alt. Bertram/Bertrand)

Old English, meaning 'illustrious'.

Berton

Old English, meaning 'bright settlement'.

Bevan

Welsh, meaning 'son of Evan'.

Bilal

Arabic, meaning 'wetting, refreshing'.

Bill

(alt. Billy)

English, from William, meaning 'determined' or 'resolute'.

Birch

Old English, meaning 'bright' or 'shining'.

B

Birger
Norwegian, meaning 'rescue'.

Bishop
Old English, meaning 'bishop'.

Bjorn
Old Norse, meaning 'bear'.

Bladen
Hebrew, meaning 'hero'.

Blaine
Irish Gaelic, meaning 'yellow'.

Blair
English, meaning 'plain'.

Blaise
French, meaning 'lisp' or 'stutter'.

Blake
Old English, meaning 'dark, black'.

Blas
(alt. Blaze)
German, meaning 'firebrand'.

Bo
Scandinavian, short form of Robert, meaning 'bright fame'.

Boaz
Hebrew, meaning 'swiftness' or 'strength'.

Bob
(alt. Bobby)
From Robert, meaning 'bright fame'.

Boden
(alt. Bodie)
Scandinavian, meaning 'shelter'.

Bogumil
Slavic, meaning 'God favour'.

Bond
Old English, meaning 'peasant farmer'.

Boris
Slavic, meaning 'battle glory'.

Bosten
English, meaning 'town by the woods'.

B

Saints' names

Anselm
Bartholomew
Francis
Gabriel
Gregory
Jerome
Nicholas
Philip
Stephen
Thomas

Bowen
Welsh, meaning 'son of Owen'.

Boyd
Scottish Gaelic, meaning 'yellow'.

Brad
(alt. Bradley)
Old English, meaning 'broad' or 'wide'.

Brady
Irish, meaning 'large-chested'.

Bradyn
Gaelic, meaning 'descendant of Bradan'.

Bram
Gaelic, meaning 'raven'.

Brandon
Old English, meaning 'gorse'.

Brandt
Old English, meaning 'beacon'.

Brandy
English, meaning 'brandy'.

Brannon
Gaelic, meaning 'raven'.

Branson
English, meaning 'son of Brand'.

Brant
Old English, meaning 'hill'.

Braulio
Greek, meaning 'shining'.

Brendan
Gaelic, meaning 'prince'.

Brennan
Gaelic, meaning 'teardrop'.

B

Brenton

English, from Brent, meaning 'hill'.

Brett

English, meaning 'a Breton'.

Brian

Gaelic, meaning 'high' or 'noble'.

Brice

Latin, meaning 'speckled'.

Brier

French, meaning 'heather'.

Brock

Old English, meaning 'badger'.

Broderick

English, meaning 'ruler'.

Brody

Gaelic, meaning both 'ditch' and 'brother'.

Brogan

Irish, meaning 'sturdy shoe'.

Bronwyn

Welsh, meaning 'white breasted'.

Brook

English, meaning 'stream'.

Bruce

Scottish, meaning 'high' or 'noble'.

Bruno

Germanic, meaning 'brown'.

Bryant

English variant of Brian, meaning 'high' or 'noble'.

Bryce

Scottish, meaning 'of Britain'.

Brycen

Scottish, meaning 'son of Bryce'.

Bryden

Irish, meaning 'strong one'.

Bryson

Welsh, meaning 'descendant of Brice'.

B

Bubba

American, meaning 'boy'.

Buck

American, meaning 'goat' or 'deer'.

Bud

(alt. Buddy)

American, meaning 'friend'.

Burdett

Middle English, meaning 'bird'.

Burke

French, meaning 'fortified settlement'.

Burl

French, meaning 'knotty wood'.

Buzz

Amercian, shortened form of Busby. Associated with the astronaut Buzz Aldrin.

Byron

Old English, meaning 'barn'. Made famous by the poet Lord Byron.

Popular African names for boys and girls

Abiba
Chike
Ebere
Faizah
Fola
Jelani
Kanene
Keisha
Razi
Salim

C Boys' names

Cabot

Old English, meaning 'to sail'.

Cade

(alt. Caden)

English, meaning 'round/lumpy'.

Cadence

Latin, meaning 'with rhythm'.

Cadogan

Welsh, meaning 'battle glory and honour'.

Caedmon

Celtic, meaning 'wise warrior'.

Caelan

Gaelic, from St Columba.

Caerwyn

(alt. Carwyn, Gerwyn)

Welsh, meaning 'white fort' or 'settlement'.

Caesar

Latin, meaning 'head of hair'. Made famous by the first Roman emperor Julius Caesar.

Caetano

Portuguese, meaning 'from Gaeta, Italy'

Caiden

Arabic, meaning 'companion'.

C

Caillou
French, meaning 'pebble'.

Cain
Biblical, brother of Abel.

Cainan
Biblical, meaning 'possessor' or 'purchaser'.

Cairo
Egyptian city.

Cal
Short form of names beginning Cal-.

Calder
Scottish, meaning 'rough waters'.

Caleb
Hebrew, meaning 'dog'.

Calen
From Caleb, meaning 'dog'.

Calix
Greek, meaning 'very handsome'.

Callahan
Irish, meaning 'contention' or 'strife'.

Callum
Gaelic, meaning 'dove'.

Calvin
French, meaning 'little bald one'.

Camden
Gaelic, meaning 'winding valley'. Also an area of north London.

Cameron
Scottish Gaelic, meaning 'crooked nose'.

Camillo
Latin, meaning 'free born' or 'noble'.

Campbell
Scottish Gaelic, meaning 'crooked mouth'.

Canaan
Biblical, meaning 'to be humbled'.

C

Candido

Latin, meaning 'candid' or 'honest'.

Cannon

French, meaning 'of the church'.

Canton

French, 'dweller of corner'. Also name given to areas of Switzerland.

Cappy

Italian, meaning 'lucky'.

Carden

Old English, meaning 'wood carder'.

Carey

Gaelic, meaning 'love'.

Carl

Old Norse, meaning 'free man'.

Carlo

Italian form of Carl, meaning 'free man'.

Carlos

Spanish form of Carl, meaning 'free man'.

Carlton

Old English, meaning 'free peasant settlement'.

Carmelo

Latin, meaning 'garden' or 'orchard'.

Carmen

Latin/Spanish, meaning 'song'.

Carmine

Latin, meaning 'song'.

Carnell

English, meaning 'defender of the castle'.

Carson

(alt. Carsten)

Scottish, meaning 'marsh-dwellers'.

Carter

Old English, meaning 'transporter of goods'.

C

Cary

Old Celtic river name. Also means 'love'.

Case
(alt. Casey)

Irish Gaelic, meaning 'alert' or 'watchful'.

Cash

Latin, shortened form of Cassius, meaning 'vain'.

Casimer

Slavic, meaning 'famous destroyer of peace'.

Cason

Latin, from Cassius, meaning 'empty' or 'hollow'.

Casper

Persian, meaning 'treasurer'.

Caspian

From the Caspian Sea.

Cassidy

Gaelic, meaning 'curly haired'.

Cassius
(alt. Cassio)

Latin, meaning 'empty, hollow'.

Cathal

Celtic, meaning 'battle rule'.

Cato

Latin, meaning 'all-knowing'.

TV personality names

Ant/hony (McPartlin)
Bruce (Forsyth)
Dec/lan (Donnelly)
Dermot (O'Leary)
Graham (Norton)
James (Corden)
Jeremy (Clarkson, Kyle, Paxman)
Russell (Brand)
Simon (Cowell)
Vernon (Kay)

C

Cecil

Latin, meaning 'blind'.

Cedar

English name of evergreen trees.

Cedric

Welsh, meaning 'spectacular bounty'.

Celestino

Spanish/Italian meaning 'heavenly'.

Chad
(alt. Chadrick)

Old English, meaning 'warlike, warrior'.

Chaim

Hebrew, meaning 'life'.

Champion

English, from the word 'champion'.

Chance

English, from the word 'chance'.

Chandler

Old English, meaning 'candle maker and seller'.

Charles
(alt. Charlie)

Old German, meaning 'free man'.

Chaska

Native American name usually given to first son.

Che

Spanish, shortened form of Jose. Made famous by Che Guevara.

Chesley

Old English, meaning 'camp on the meadow'.

Chester

Latin, meaning 'camp of soldiers'.

Chima

Old English, meaning 'hilly land'.

C

Christian

English, from the word Christian.

Christophe

French variant of Christopher, meaning 'bearing Christ inside'.

Christopher

Greek, meaning 'bearing Christ inside'.

Cian

Irish, meaning 'ancient'.

Ciaran

Irish, meaning 'black'.

Cicero

Latin, meaning 'chickpea'. Famous Roman philosopher and orator.

Cimarron

City in western Kansas.

Ciprian

Latin, meaning 'from Cyprus'.

Ciro

Spanish, meaning 'sun'.

Clancy

Old Irish, meaning 'red warrior'.

Clarence

Latin, meaning 'one who lives near the river Clare'.

Clark

Latin, meaning 'clerk'.

Claude

(alt. Claudie, Claudio, Claudius)

Latin, meaning 'lame'.

Claus

Variant of Nicholas, meaning 'people of victory'.

Clay

English, from the word clay.

Clement

(alt. Clem)

Latin, meaning 'merciful'.

Cleo
Greek, meaning 'glory'.

Cletus
Greek, meaning 'illustrious'.

Cliff
(alt. Clifford, Clifton)
English, from the word cliff.

Clint
(alt. Clinton)
Old English, meaning 'fenced settlement'.

Clive
English, meaning 'cliff'.

Clyde
Scottish, from the river in Glasgow.

Coby
(alt. Cody, Colby)
Irish, son of Oda.

Colden
Old English, meaning 'dark valley'.

C

Cole
Old French, meaning 'coal black'.

Coley
Old English, meaning 'coal black'.

Colin
Gaelic, meaning 'young creature'.

Colson
Old English, meaning 'coal black'.

Colton
English, meaning 'swarthy'.

Columbus
Latin, meaning 'dove'.

Colwyn
Welsh place name.

Conan
Gaelic, meaning 'wolf'.

Conley
Gaelic, meaning 'sensible'.

C

Connell
(alt. Connolly)
Irish, meaning 'high' or 'mighty'.

Connor
(alt. Conrad, Conroy)
Irish, meaning 'lover of hounds'.

Constant
(alt. Constantine)
English, from the word constant.

Cooper

Uncommon three syllable names

Alastair
Barnaby
Dominic
Elijah
Elliot
Gideon
Nathaniel
Reginald
Theodore

Old English, meaning 'barrel maker'.

Corban
Hebrew, meaning 'dedicated and belonging to God'.

Corbett
(alt. Corbin, Corby)
Norman French, meaning 'young crow'.

Cordell
Old English, meaning 'cord maker'.

Corey
Gaelic, meaning 'hill hollow'.

Corin
Latin, meaning 'spear'.

Cormac
Gaelic, meaning 'impure son'.

Cornelius
(alt. Cornell)
Latin, meaning 'horn'.

C

Cortez

Spanish, meaning 'courteous'.

Corwin

Old English, meaning 'heart's friend' or 'companion'.

Cosimo

(alt. Cosme, Cosmo)

Italian, meaning 'order' or 'beauty'.

Coty

French, meaning 'riverbank'.

Coulter

English, meaning 'young horse'.

Courtney

Old English, meaning 'domain of Curtis'.

Cowan

Gaelic, meaning 'hollow in the hill'.

Craig

Welsh, meaning 'rock'.

Crispin

Latin, meaning 'curly haired'.

Croix

French, meaning 'cross'.

Cruz

Spanish, meaning 'cross'. Made famous by David and Victoria Beckham's son.

Curran

Gaelic, meaning 'dagger' or 'hero'.

Curtis

(alt. Curt)

Old French, meaning 'courteous'.

Cutler

Old English, meaning 'knife maker'.

Cyprian

English, meaning 'from Cyprus'.

Cyril

Greek, meaning 'master' or 'Lord'.

Cyrus

Persian, meaning 'Lord'.

Popular American names for boys and girls

Aubree
Brayden
Cooper
Grayson
Kayla
Kendra
Lacey
Landon
Misty
Peyton

# D

Boys' names

Dafydd

Welsh, meaning 'beloved'.
Made famous by the character
in the BBC television series
Little Britain.

Daichi

Japanese, meaning 'great
wisdom'.

Daisuke

Japanese, meaning
'lionhearted'.

Dakari

African, meaning 'happy'.

Dale

Old English, meaning 'valley'.

Dallin

English, meaning 'dweller in the
valley'.

Dalton

English, meaning 'town in the
valley'.

Daly

Gaelic, meaning 'assembly'.

Damarion

Greek, meaning 'gentle'.

Damian

(alt. Damon)

Greek, meaning 'to tame/
subdue'.

D

Dane
Old English, meaning 'from Denmark'.

Daniel
(alt. Dan, Danny)
Hebrew, meaning 'God is my judge'.

Dante
Latin, meaning 'lasting'. Famous Italian 13th century poet Dante Alighieri.

Darby
Irish, meaning 'without envy'.

Darcy
Gaelic, meaning 'dark'. Associated with Jane Austen's Mr Darcy, and the parody of this character in *Bridget Jones' Diary*.

Dario
(alt. Darius)
Greek, meaning 'Kingly'.

Darnell
Old English, meaning 'the hidden spot'.

Darragh
Irish, meaning 'dark oak'.

Darrell
(alt. Daryl)
Old English, meaning 'open'.

Darren
(alt. Darrian)
Gaelic, meaning 'great'.

Darrick
Old German, meaning 'power of the tribe'.

Darshan
Hindi, meaning 'vision'.

Darwin
Old English, meaning 'dear friend'.

Dash
(alt. Dashawn)
American, meaning 'enlightened one'.

Dashiell
French, meaning 'page boy'.

D

David
(alt. Dave, Davey, Davie, Davian)
Biblical, meaning 'beloved'.

Davis
Old English, meaning 'son of David'.

Dawson
Old English, meaning 'son of David'.

Dax
(alt. Daxton)
French origin, was once a town in southwestern France. Now associated with the *Star Trek* character.

Dayal
Indian, meaning 'kind'.

Dayton
Old English, meaning 'David's place'.

Dean
Old English, meaning 'valley'.

Declan
Irish, meaning 'full of goodness'.

Dedric
Old English, meaning 'gifted ruler'.

Deepak
(alt. Deepan)
Indian, meaning 'illumination'.

Del
(alt. Delano, Delbert, Dell)
Old English, meaning 'bright shining one'.

Demetrius
Greek, meaning 'harvest lover'.

Dempsey
Irish, meaning 'proud'.

Denham
(alt. Denholm)
Old English, meaning 'valley settlement'.

Dennis
(alt. Denny, Denton)
English, meaning 'follower of Dionysius'.

D

Old name, new fashion?

Augustus
Bertrand
Edger
Felix
Gilbert
Hector
Jasper
Norris
Percival
Reginald
Sebastian
Theodore
Winston

Denver
City in Colorado, USA.

Denzil
English, town in Cornwall.

Deon
Greek, meaning 'of Zeus'.

Derek
English, meaning 'power of the tribe'.

Dermot
Irish, meaning 'free man'.

Desmond
Irish, meaning 'from south Munster'.

Destin
French, meaning 'destiny'.

Devyn
Irish, meaning 'poet'.

Dewey
Welsh origin, from Dewi (David).

Dexter
(alt. Dex)
Latin, meaning 'right-handed'.

Dick
(alt. Dickie, Dickon)
From Richard, meaning 'powerful leader'.

Didier
French, meaning 'much desired'.

Diego
Spanish, meaning 'supplanter'.

D

Dietrich
Old German, meaning 'power of the tribe'.

Diggory
English, meaning 'dyke'.

Dilbert
English, meaning 'day-bright'.

Dimitri
(alt. Dimitrios, Dimitris)
Greek, meaning 'Prince'.

Dino
Diminutive of Dean, meaning 'valley'.

Dion
Greek, short form of Dionysius.

Dirk
Variant of Derek, meaning 'power of the tribe'.

Dobbin
Diminutive of Robert, meaning 'bright fame'.

Dominic
Latin, meaning 'Lord'.

Donald
(alt. Don, Donal, Donaldo)
Gaelic, meaning 'great chief'.

Donato
Italian, meaning 'gift'.

Donnell
(alt. Donnie, Donny)
Gaelic, meaning 'world fighter'.

Donovan
Gaelic, meaning 'dark-haired chief'.

Doran
Gaelic, meaning 'exile'.

Dorian
Greek, meaning 'descendant of Doris'.

Dorsey
From the French D'Orsay.

Douglas
(alt. Dougal, Dougie)
Scottish, meaning 'black river'.

D

Draco

Latin, meaning 'dragon'. Made popular by the character Draco Malfoy in the *Harry Potter* novels.

Drake

Greek origin, meaning 'dragon'.

Drew

Shortened form of Andrew, meaning 'man' or 'warrior'.

Dudley

Old English, meaning 'people's field'. Also a town in the West Midlands, and the name of Harry Potter's cousin.

Duff

Gaelic, meaning 'swarthy'.

Duke

Latin origin, meaning 'leader'.

Duncan

Scottish, meaning 'dark warrior'.

Dustin
(alt. Dusty)

French origin, meaning 'brave warrior'.

Dwayne

Irish Gaelic origin, meaning 'swarthy'.

Dwight

Flemish, meaning 'blond'.

Dwyer

Gaelic, meaning 'dark wise one'.

Dylan
(alt. Dillon)

Welsh, meaning 'son of the sea'.

E

Boys' names

Eamon
(alt. Eames)

Irish, meaning 'wealthy protector'.

Earl
(alt. Earle, Errol)

English, from the word Earl.

Ebb
Short form of Ebenezer, meaning 'stone of help'.

Ebenezer
Hebrew, meaning 'stone of help'.

Ed
(alt. Edd, Eddie, Eddy)

Shortened form of Edward, meaning 'wealthy guard'.

Edgar
(alt.Elgar)

Old English, meaning 'wealthy spear'.

Edison
English, meaning 'son of Edward'.

Edmund
English, meaning 'wealthy protector'.

Edric
Old English, meaning 'rich and powerful'.

Edsel
Old German, meaning 'noble'.

E

Edward
(alt. Eduardo)
Old English, meaning 'wealthy guard'.

Edwin
English, meaning 'wealthy friend'.

Efrain
Hebrew, meaning 'fruitful'.

Egan
Irish, meaning 'fire'.

Einar
Old Norse, meaning 'battle leader'.

Eladio
Greek, meaning 'Greek'.

Elam
Hebrew, meaning 'eternal'.

Elbert
Old English, meaning 'famous'.

Eldon
Old English, meaning 'Ella's hill'.

Eldred
(alt. Eldridge)
Old English, meaning 'old venerable counsel'.

Elgin
Old English, meaning 'high minded'.

Eli
(alt. Eliah)
Hebrew, meaning 'high'.

Elias
(alt. Elijah)
Hebrew, meaning 'the Lord is my God'.

Elio
Spanish origin, meaning 'the Lord is my God'.

Ellery
Old English, meaning 'elder tree'.

E

Elliott

Variant of Elio, meaning 'the Lord is my God'.

Ellis

Welsh variant of Elio, meaning 'the Lord is my God'.

Ellison

English, meaning 'son of Ellis'.

Elmer

(alt. Elmo)

Old English, meaning 'noble'.

Elon

Hebrew, meaning 'oak tree'.

Elroy

French, meaning 'king'.

Elton

Old English, meaning 'Ella's town'.

Elvin

English, meaning 'elf-like'.

Elvis

Figure in Norse mythology. Made famous by the singer Elvis Presley.

Emanuel

Hebrew, meaning 'God is with us'.

Emeric

German, meaning 'work rule'.

Emile

(alt. Emiliano, Emilio)

Latin, meaning 'eager'.

Emlyn

Welsh, name of town, Newcastle Emlyn, in West Wales.

Emmett

English origin, meaning 'universal'.

Emrys

Welsh, meaning 'immortal'.

Enoch

Hebrew, meaning 'dedicated'.

E

Enrico
(alt. Enrique)

Form of Henry, meaning 'home ruler'.

Enzo

Italian, short for Lorenzo, meaning 'laurel'.

Eoghan
(alt. Eoin)

Irish form of Owen, meaning 'well born' or 'noble'.

Ephron
(alt. Effron)

Biblical, meaning 'dust'.

Erasmo
(alt. Erasmus)

Greek, meaning 'to love'.

Eric

Old Norse, meaning 'ruler'.

Ernest
(alt. Ernesto, Ernie, Ernst)

Old German, meaning 'serious'.

Erskine

Scottish, meaning 'high cliff'.

Erwin

Old English, meaning 'boar friend'.

Ethan
(alt. Etienne)

Hebrew, meaning 'long lived'.

Eugene

Greek, meaning 'well-born'.

Evan

Welsh, meaning 'God is good'.

Everard

Old English, meaning 'strong boar'.

Everett

English, meaning 'strong boar'.

Ewald
(alt. Ewan, Ewell)

From Owen, meaning 'well born' or 'noble'.

Ezra

Hebrew, meaning 'helper'.

F

Boys' names

Fabian
(alt. Fabien, Fabio)
Latin, meaning 'one who grows beans'.

Fabrice
(alt. Fabrizio)
Latin origin, meaning 'works with his hands'.

Faisal
Arabic, meaning 'resolute'.

Faron
Spanish, meaning 'pharaoh'.

Farrell
Gaelic, meaning 'hero'.

Faulkner
Latin, from 'falcon'.

Faustino
Latin, meaning 'fortunate'.

Felix
(alt. Felice)
Italian/Latin, meaning 'happy'.

Felipe
(alt. Filippo)
Spanish, meaning 'lover of horses'.

Fennel
Latin, name of a herb.

F

Names of poets

Alfred (Lord Tennyson)
Allen (Ginsberg)
Dylan (Thomas)
Geoffrey (Chaucer)
Kingsley (Amis)
Langston (Hughes)
Ralph (Waldo Emerson)
Robert (Burns)
Seamus (Heaney)
William (Wordsworth)

Ferdinand
(alt. Fernando)

Old German, meaning 'bold voyager'.

Fergus
(alt. Ferguson)

Gaelic, meaning 'supreme man'.

Ferris

Gaelic, meaning 'rock'.

Fidel

Latin, meaning 'faithful'.

Finbar

Gaelic, meaning 'fair head'.

Finian

Gaelic, meaning 'fair'.

Finlay
(alt. Finley, Finn)

Gaelic, meaning 'fair haired courageous one'.

Finnegan

Gaelic, meaning 'fair'.

Fintan

Gaelic, meaning 'little fair one'.

Flavio

Latin, meaning 'yellow hair'.

F

Florencio
(alt. Florentino)
Latin, meaning 'from Florence'.

Florian
(alt. Florin)
Slavic/Latin, meaning 'flower'.

Floyd
Welsh origin, meaning 'grey haired'.

Flynn
Gaelic, meaning 'with a ruddy complexion'.

Fortunato
Italian, meaning 'lucky'.

Foster
Old English, meaning 'woodsman'.

Fotini
(alt. Fotis)
Greek, meaning 'light'.

Francesco
(alt. Francis, Francisco, Franco, François)
Latin, meaning 'from France'.

Frank
(alt. Frankie, Franklin, Franz)
Middle English, meaning 'free landholder'.

Fraser
Scottish, meaning 'of the forest men'.

Fred
(alt. Freddie, Frederick)
Old German, meaning 'peaceful ruler'.

Furman
Old German, meaning 'ferryman'.

G

Boys' names

Gabe

Shortened form of Gabriel, meaning 'hero of God'.

Gabino

Latin origin, meaning 'God is my strength'.

Gabriel

Hebrew, meaning 'hero of God'. One of the archangels.

Gael

English, old reference to the Celts.

Gaetano

Italian, from the name of a region in southern Italy.

Galen

Greek origin, meaning 'healer'.

Galileo

Italian, meaning 'from Galilee'.

Ganesh

Hindi, meaning 'Lord of the throngs'. One of the Hindu deities.

Gannon

Irish, meaning 'fair skinned'.

Gareth
(alt. Garth)

Welsh, meaning 'gentle'.

G

Garfield

Old English, meaning 'spear field'. Also the name of the cartoon cat.

Garland

English, as in 'garland of flowers'.

Garnet

English, precious stone red in colour.

Garry
(alt. Gary, Geary)

Old English, meaning 'spear'.

Gaspar
(alt. Gaspard)

Persian, meaning 'treasurer'.

Gaston

From the region in the south of France.

Gavin
(alt. Gawain)

Scottish/Welsh, meaning 'little falcon'.

Gene

Shortened form of Eugene, meaning 'well born'.

Gennaro

Italian, meaning 'of Janus'.

Geoffrey

Old German, meaning 'peace'.

George
(alt. Giorgio)

Greek, meaning 'farmer'.

Gerald
(alt. Geraldo, Gerard, Gerardo, Gerhard)

Old German, meaning 'spear ruler'.

Geronimo

Italian origin, meaning 'sacred name'.

Gerry

English, meaning 'independent'.

Gert

Old German, meaning 'strong spear'.

G

Gervase
Old German, meaning 'with honour'.

Giacomo
Italian, meaning 'God's son'.

Gibson
English, meaning 'son of Gilbert'.

Gideon
Hebrew, meaning 'tree cutter'.

Gilbert
(alt. Gilberto)
French, meaning 'bright promise'.

Giles
Greek, meaning 'small goat'.

Gino
Italian, meaning 'well born'.

Giovanni
Italian form of John, meaning 'God is gracious'.

Giulio
Italian, meaning 'youthful'.

Giuseppe
Italian form of Joseph, meaning 'Jehovah increases'.

Glen
English, from the word 'glen'.

Glyn
Welsh form of Glen.

Godfrey
German, meaning 'peace of God'.

Gordon
Gaelic, meaning 'large fortification'.

Names from ancient Rome

Brutus
Caesar
Julius
Lucius
Marcus
Maximus
Nero
Rufus
Titus

G

Gottlieb
German, meaning 'good love'.

Gower
Area on the Welsh coast.

Graeme
(alt. Graham)
English, meaning 'gravelled area'.

Grant
English, from the word 'grant'.

Granville
English, meaning 'gravelly town'.

Gray
(alt. Grey)
English, from the word 'gray'.

Grayson
English, meaning 'son of gray'.

Green
English, from the word 'green'.

Greg
(alt. Gergorio, Gregory, Grieg)
English, meaning 'watcher'.

Griffin
English, from the word 'griffin'.

Guido
Italian, meaning 'guide'.

Guillaume
French form of William, meaning 'strong protector'.

Gulliver
English, meaning 'glutton'.

Gunther
German, meaning 'warrior'.

Gurpreet
Indian, meaning 'love of the teacher'.

Gustave
(alt. Gus)
Scandinavian, royal staff.

Guy
English, from the word 'guy'.

Gwyn
Welsh, meaning 'white'.

 **Boys' names**

Habib

Arabic, meaning 'beloved one'.

Haden

(alt. Haiden)

English, meaning 'hedged valley'.

Hades

Greek, meaning 'sightless'. Name of the underworld in Greek mythology.

Hadrian

From Hadria, a north Italian city.

Hadwin

Old English, meaning 'friend in war'.

Hakeem

Arabic, meaning 'wise and insightful'.

Hal

(alt. Hale, Hallie)

English, nickname for Henry, meaning 'home ruler'.

Hamid

Arabic, meaning 'praiseworthy'.

Hamilton

Old English, meaning 'flat topped hill'.

Hamish

Scottish form of James, meaning 'he who supplants'.

H

Hampus

Swedish form of Homer, meaning 'pledge'.

Hamza

Arabic, meaning 'lamb'.

Han

(alt. Hannes, Hans)

Scandinavian, meaning 'the Lord is gracious'.

Hank

German, meaning 'home ruler'. Form of Henry.

Hansel

German, meaning 'the Lord is gracious'.

Hardy

English, meaning 'tough'.

Harlan

English, meaning 'dweller by the boundary wood'.

Harland

Old English, meaning 'army land'.

Harley

Old English, meaning 'hare meadow'.

Harmon

Old German, meaning 'soldier'.

Harold

Scandinavian, meaning 'army ruler'.

Harry

Old German, meaning 'home ruler'. Form of Henry.

Hart

Old English, meaning 'stag'.

Names from ancient Greece

Aesop
Demetrius
Erasmus
Georgios
Homer
Jason
Lysandos
Nikolaos
Pyrrhus
Theodore

H

Harvey

Old English, meaning 'strong and worthy'.

Haskell

Hebrew, meaning 'intellect'.

Hassan

Arabic, meaning 'handsome'.

Haydn

Old English, meaning 'hedged valley'.

Heart

English, from the word 'heart'.

Heath

English, meaning 'heath' or 'moor'.

Heathcliff

English, meaning 'cliff near a heath'. Made famous by Emily Bronte's novel *Wuthering Heights*.

Heber

Hebrew, meaning 'partner'.

Hector

Greek, meaning 'steadfast'.

Henry

(alt. Henri, Hendrik, Hendrix)

Old German, meaning 'home ruler'.

Henson

English, meaning 'son of Henry'.

Herbert

(alt. Bert, Herb)

Old German, meaning 'illustrious warrior'.

Heriberto

Italian variant of Herbert, meaning 'illustrious warrior'.

Herman

(alt. Herminio, Hermon)

Old German, meaning 'soldier'.

Hermes

Greek, meaning 'messenger'.

Herschel

Yiddish, meaning 'deer'.

H

Hezekiah

Biblical, meaning 'God gives strength'.

Hideki

Japanese, meaning 'excellent trees'.

Hideo

Japanese, meaning 'excellent name'.

Hilario

Latin, meaning 'cheerful, happy'.

Hilary

English, meaning 'cheerful'.

Hillel

Hebrew, meaning 'greatly praised'.

Hilliard

Old German, meaning 'battle guard'.

Hilton

Old English, meaning 'hill settlement'.

Hiram

Hebrew, meaning 'exalted brother'.

Hiro

From Spanish, meaning 'sacred name'.

Hiroshi

Japanese, meaning 'generous'.

Hirsch

Yiddish, meaning 'deer'.

Hobart

English, meaning 'bright and shining intellect'.

Hodge

English, meaning 'son of Roger'.

Hogan

Gaelic, meaning 'youth'.

Holden

English, meaning 'deep valley'.

Hollis

Old English, meaning 'holly tree'.

Homer

Greek, meaning 'pledge'.

Honorius

Latin, meaning 'honourable'.

Horace

Latin, name of the Roman poet.

Houston

Old English, meaning 'Hugh's town'. Also city in the state of Texas, USA.

Howard

Old English, meaning 'noble watchman'.

Howell

Welsh, meaning 'eminent and remarkable'.

Hoyt

Norse, meaning 'spirit' or 'soul'.

Hristo

From Christo, meaning 'follower of Christ'.

Hubert

German, meaning 'bright and shining intellect'.

Hudson

Old English, meaning 'son of Hugh'.

Hugh

Old German, meaning 'soul, mind and intellect'.

Humbert

Old German, meaning 'famous giant'. Be warned: it's the name and surname of the paedophile protagonist of Vladimir Nabokov's *Lolita*.

Humphrey

Old German, meaning 'peaceful warrior'.

Hunter

English, from the word 'hunter'.

Hurley

Gaelic, meaning 'sea tide'.

H

Huxley

Old English, meaning 'Hugh's meadow'.

Hyrum

Hebrew, meaning 'exalted brother'.

Names with positive meanings

Auden – Friend
Basim – Smile
Dustin – Brave
Ervin – Beautiful
Gene – Noble
Jamal – Handsome
Jay – Happy
Pradeep – Light
Tate – Cheerful
Tova – Good

Boys' names

Iago
Spanish, meaning 'he who supplants'.

Ian
(alt. Ion)
Variant of John, meaning 'God is gracious'.

Ianto
Welsh, meaning 'gift of God'.

Ibrahim
Arabic, meaning 'father of many'.

Ichabod
Hebrew, meaning 'glory is good'.

Ichiro
Japanese, meaning 'first born son'.

Girls' names for boys (male spellings)

Darcy
Jean
Kay
Kelly
Kelsey
Madison
Nat
Paris
Sandy
Sasha

I

Idris
Welsh, meaning 'fiery leader'.

Ifan
Welsh variant of John, meaning 'God is gracious'.

Ignacio
Latin, meaning 'ardent' or 'burning'.

Ignatz
German, meaning 'fiery'.

Igor
Russian, meaning 'Ing's soldier'.

Ikaika
Hawaiian, meaning 'strong'.

Ike
Hebrew, short for Isaac, meaning 'laughter'.

Ilan
Hebrew, meaning 'tree'.

Ilias
Variant of Hebrew Elijah, meaning 'the Lord is my God'.

Imanol
Hebrew, meaning 'God is with us'.

Indiana
Latin, meaning 'from India'. Also a state in the US.

Indigo
English, describing a deep blue colour.

Ingo
Danish, meaning 'meadow'.

Inigo
Spanish, meaning 'fiery'.

Ioannis
Greek, meaning 'the Lord is gracious'.

Ira
Hebrew, meaning 'full grown and watchful'.

Irvin
(alt. Irving, Irwin)
Gaelic, meaning 'green and fresh water'.

Isaac
(alt. Isaak)

Hebrew, meaning 'laughter'.

Isadore
(alt. Isidore, Isidro)

Greek, meaning 'gift of Isis'.

Isai
(alt. Isaiah, Isaias, Izaiah)

Arabic, meaning 'protection and security'.

Iser

Yiddish, meaning 'God wrestler'.

Ishmael
(alt. Ismael)

Hebrew, meaning 'God listens'.

Israel

Hebrew, meaning 'God perseveres'. Also the name of the country.

Istvan

Hungarian variant of Stephen, meaning 'crowned'.

Place names

Aidrian
Ainsley
Ashton
Bradley
Bruce
Emlyn
Glen
Tay
Wade
Wesley

Itai

Hebrew, meaning 'the Lord is with me'.

Ivan

Hebrew, meaning 'God is gracious'.

Ivanhoe

Russian origin, meaning 'God is gracious'. Also name of the novel by Walter Scott.

Ivey

English, variant of Ivy.

Ivo

From the French yves, meaning 'yew tree'.

125

Ivor

Scandinavian, meaning 'yew'.

Ivory

English, from the word ivory.

Long names

Alexander
Bartholomew
Christopher
Demetrius
Giovanni
Maximillian
Montgomery
Nathaniel
Sebastian
Zachariah

J Boys' names

Jabari
Swahili, meaning 'valiant'.

Jabez
Hebrew, meaning 'borne in pain'.

Jace
(alt. Jaece, Jase, Jayce)
Hebrew, meaning 'healer'.

Jacek
African, meaning 'hyacinth'.

Jacinto
African, meaning 'hyacinth'.

Jack
(alt. Jackie, Jacky)
From the Hebrew John, meaning 'God is gracious'.

Jackson
English, meaning 'son of Jack'.

Jaco
From the Hebrew Jacob, meaning 'he who supplants'.

Jacob
(alt. Jacobo, Jago)
Hebrew, meaning 'he who supplants'.

Jacques
French form of Jack, meaning 'God is gracious'.

J

Jaden
(alt. Jaden, Jadyn, Jaeden, Jaiden, Jaidyn, Jayden, Jaydin)
Hebrew, meaning 'Jehovah has heard'.

Jafar
Arabic, meaning 'stream'.

Jagger
Old English, meaning 'one who cuts'.

Jaheem
(alt. Jaheim)
Hebrew, meaning 'raised up'.

Jahir
Hindi, meaning 'jewel'.

Jaime
Variant for James, meaning 'he who supplants'. J'aime is French for 'I love'.

Jair
(alt. Jairo)
Hebrew, meaning 'God enlightens'.

Jake
Shortened form of Jacob, meaning 'he who supplants'.

Jalen
Greek, meaning 'healer' or 'tranquil'.

Jali
Swahili, meaning 'musician'.

Jalon
Greek, meaning 'healer' or 'tranquil'.

Jamaal
(alt. Jamal)
Arabic, meaning 'handsome'.

Jamar
(alt. Jamarcus, Jamari, Jamarion, Jamir)
Modern variant of Jamal, meaning 'handsome'.

Jamel
Arabic, meaning 'handsome'.

James
English, meaning 'he who supplants'.

J

Jameson
(alt. Jamison)
English, meaning 'son of James'.

Jamie
(alt. Jamey, Jaimie)
Nickname for James, meaning 'he who supplants'.

Jamil
Arabic, meaning 'handsome'.

Jamin
Hebrew, meaning 'son of the right hand'.

Jan
(alt. Janko, János)
Slavic, from John meaning 'the Lord is gracious'.

Janus
Latin, meaning 'gateway'. Roman god of doors, beginnings and endings.

Japhet
(alt. Japheth)
Hebrew, meaning 'comely'.

Jaquez
French origin, form of Jacques, meaning 'God is gracious'.

Jared
(alt. Jarem, Jaren, Jaret, Jarod, Jarrod)
Hebrew, meaning 'descending'.

Jarlath
Gaelic, from Iarlaith, from Saint Iarfhlaith.

Jarom
Greek, meaning 'to raise and exalt'.

Short names

Al
Ben
Dai
Ed
Jay
Jon
Max
Rio
Sam
Ty

J

Jarrell
Variant of Gerald, meaning 'spear ruler'.

Jarrett
Old English, meaning 'spear-brave'.

Jarvis
Old German, meaning 'with honour'.

Jason
Greek, meaning 'healer'.

Jasper
Greek, meaning 'treasure holder'.

Javen
Arabic, meaning 'youth'.

Javier
Spanish, meaning 'bright'.

Jaxon
From Jackson, meaning 'son of Jack'.

Jay
Latin, meaning 'jaybird'.

Jaylan
Greek, meaning 'healer'.

Jeevan
Indian, meaning 'life'.

Jefferey
(alt. Jeff)
Old German, meaning 'peace'.

Jefferson
English, meaning 'son of Jeffrey'.

Jensen
Scandinavian, meaning 'son of Jan'.

Jeremy
(alt. Jem)
Hebrew, meaning 'the Lord exalts'.

Jeriah
Hebrew, meaning 'Jehovah has seen'.

Jericho
Arabic, meaning 'city of the moon'.

J

Jermaine
Latin, meaning 'brotherly'.

Jerome
Greek, meaning 'sacred name'.

Jerry
English, from Gerald, meaning 'spear ruler'.

Jesse
Hebrew, meaning 'the Lord exists'.

Jesus
Hebrew, meaning 'the Lord is Salvation' and the Son of God.

Jethro
Hebrew, meaning 'eminent'.

Jim
(alt. Jimmy)
From James, meaning 'he who supplants'.

Jiri
(alt. Jiro)
Greek, meaning 'farmer'.

Joachim
Hebrew, meaning 'established by God'.

Joah
(alt. João)
Hebrew, meaning 'God is gracious'.

Joaquin
Hebrew, meaning 'established by God'.

Joe
(alt. Joey, Johan, Johannes, Jomar)
From Joseph, meaning 'Jehovah increases'.

Joel
Hebrew, meaning 'Jehovah is the Lord'.

John
Hebrew, meaning 'the Lord is gracious'.

Johnny
(alt. Jon, Jonny)
From Jonathan, meaning 'gift of God'.

J

Jolyon

From Julian, meaning 'young'.

Jonah

Hebrew, meaning 'dove'.

Jonas

Hebrew, meaning 'dove'.

Jonathan

(alt. Johnathan, Johnathon, Jonathon, Jonty)

Hebrew, meaning 'gift from God'.

Jordan

(alt. Jory, Judd)

Hebrew, meaning 'down-flowing'.

Jorge

From George, meaning 'farmer'.

José

Spanish variant of Joseph, meaning 'Jehovah increases'.

Joseph

(alt. Joss)

Hebrew, meaning 'Jehovah increases'.

Josh

Shortened form of Joshua, meaning 'Jehovah is salvation'.

Joshua

Hebrew, meaning 'Jehovah is salvation'.

Josiah

Hebrew, meaning 'Jehovah helps'.

Josué

Spanish variant of Joshua, meaning 'Jehovah is salvation'.

Jovan

Latin, meaning 'the supreme God'.

Joyce

Latin, meaning 'joy'.

Juan

Spanish variant of John, meaning 'the Lord is gracious'.

Jubal

Hebrew, meaning 'ram's horn'.

J

'Bad boy' names

Ace
Arnie
Axel
Bruce
Buzz
Conan
Guy
Rhett
Spike
Tyson

Jude

Hebrew, meaning 'praise' or 'thanks'.

Judson

Variant of Jude, meaning 'praise' or 'thanks'.

Jules

From Julian, meaning 'Jove's child'.

Julian

Greek, meaning 'Jove's child'.

Julien

French variant of Julian, meaning 'Jove's child'.

Julio

Italian variant of Julian, meaning 'Jove's child'.

Junior

Latin, meaning 'the younger one'.

Junius

Latin, meaning 'young'.

Jupiter

Latin, meaning 'the supreme God'. Jupiter was king of the Roman gods and the god of thunder. Jupiter is also the largest planet in the solar system.

Juraj

Hebrew, meaning 'God is my judge'.

Jurgen

Greek, meaning 'farmer'.

Justice

English, from the word 'justice'.

J

Justin
(alt. Justus)

Latin, meaning 'just and upright'.

Juwan

Hebrew, meaning 'the Lord is gracious'.

Famous male guitarists

Brian (May)
Carlos (Santana)
Chuck (Berry)
Eddie (Van Halen)
Eric (Clapton)
Frank (Zappa)
Jeff (Beck)
Jimi/Jimmy (Hendrix/Page)
Joe (Satriani)
Keith (Richards)

 Boys' names

Kabelo
African, meaning 'gift'.

Kade
Scottish, meaning 'from the wetlands'.

Kadeem
Arabic, meaning 'one who serves'.

Kaden
(alt. Kadin, Kaeden, Kaedin, Kaiden)

Arabic, meaning 'companion'.

Kadir
Arabic, meaning 'capable and competent'.

Kahlil
Arabic, meaning 'friend'.

Kai
Greek, meaning 'keeper of the keys'.

Kaito
Japanese, meaning 'ocean and sake dipper'.

Kalani
Hawaiian, meaning 'sky'.

Kale
German, meaning 'free man'.

Kaleb
Hebrew, meaning 'dog' or 'aggressive'.

Kalen
Gaelic, meaning 'uncertain'.

K

Kaleo

Hawaiian, meaning 'the voice'.

Kalil

Arabic, meaning 'friend'.

Kalvin

French, meaning 'bald'.

Kamari

Indian, meaning 'the enemy of desire'.

Kamden

English, meaning 'winding valley'.

Kamil

Arabic, meaning 'perfection'.

Kane

Gaelic, meaning 'little battler'.

Kani

Hawaiian, meaning 'sound'.

Kanye

African town. Made popular by rapper Kanye West.

Kareem

(alt. Karim)

Arabic, meaning 'generous'.

Karl

(alt. Karson)

Old German, meaning 'free man'.

Kasey

Irish, meaning 'alert'.

Kaspar

Persian, meaning 'treasurer'.

Kavon

Gaelic, meaning 'handsome'.

Kayden

Arabic, meaning 'companion'.

Kazimierz

Polish, meaning 'declares peace'.

Kazuki

Japanese, meaning 'radiant hope'.

K

Kazuo

Japanese, meaning 'harmonious man'.

Keagan

(alt. Keegan, Kegan)
Gaelic, meaning 'small flame'.

Keane

Gaelic, meaning 'fighter'.

Keanu

Hawaiian, meaning 'breeze'.

Keary

Gaelic, meaning 'black-haired'.

Keaton

English, meaning 'place of hawks'.

Keeler

Gaelic, meaning 'beautiful and graceful'.

Keenan

(alt. Kenan)
Gaelic, meaning 'little ancient one'.

Keiji

Japanese, meaning 'govern with discretion'.

Keir

Gaelic, meaning 'dark-haired' or 'dark-skinned'.

Keith

Gaelic, meaning 'woodland'.

Kekoa

Hawaiian, meaning 'brave one' or 'soldier'.

Kelby

Old English, meaning 'farmhouse near the stream'.

Kell

(alt. Kellan, Kellen, Kelley, Kelly, Kiel)
Norse, meaning 'spring'.

Kelsey

Old English, meaning 'victorious ship'.

Kelton

Old English, meaning 'town of the keels'.

137

K

Kelvin
Old English, meaning 'friend of ships'.

Ken
Shortened form of Kenneth, meaning 'born of fire'.

Kendal
Old English, meaning 'the Kent river valley'.

Kendon
Old English, meaning 'brave guard'.

Kendrick
Gaelic, meaning 'royal ruler'.

Kenelm
Old English, meaning 'bold'.

Kenji
Japanese, meaning 'intelligent second son'.

Kennedy
Gaelic, meaning 'helmet head'.

Kenneth
(alt. Kenney)
Gaelic, meaning 'born of fire'.

Kennison
English, meaning 'son of Kenneth'.

Kent
From the English county.

Kenton
English, meaning 'town of Ken'.

Kenya
From the country in Africa.

Kenyatta
From Kenya.

Kenyon
From Kenya.

Kenzo
Japanese, meaning 'wise'.

Keola
Hawaiian, meaning 'life'.

Keon
(alt. Keoni)
Hawaiian, meaning 'gracious'.

Kepler
German, meaning 'hat maker'.

Kermit
(alt. Kerwin)

Gaelic, meaning 'without envy'. Associated with Kermit the Frog, the Muppets character.

Kerr

English, meaning 'wetland'.

Keshav

Indian, meaning 'beautiful-haired'.

Kevin

Gaelic, meaning 'handsome beloved'.

Khalid
(alt. Khalif, Khalil)

Arabic, meaning 'immortal'.

Kian
(alt. Keyon, Kyan)

Irish, meaning 'ancient'.

Kiefer

German, meaning 'barrel maker'.

Kieran
(alt. Kyron)

Gaelic, meaning 'black'.

Kijana

African, meaning 'youth'.

Kilby

From the English Cilebi, a place in Leicestershire.

Kilian

Irish, meaning 'bright headed'.

Kimani

African, meaning 'beautiful and sweet'.

King

English, from the word 'king'.

Kingsley

English, meaning 'the king's meadow'.

Kirby

German, meaning 'settlement by a church'.

Kirk

Old German, meaning 'church'.

Klaus

German, meaning 'victorious'.

K

Kobe
(alt. Koda, Kody)
Japanese, meaning 'a Japanese city'.

Kofi
Ghanaian, meaning 'born on Friday'.

Kohana
Japanese, meaning 'little flower'.

Kojo
Ghanaian, meaning 'Monday'.

Kolby
Norse, meaning 'settlement'.

Korbin
Gaelic, meaning 'a steep hill'.

Kramer
German, meaning 'shopkeeper'.

Kris
(alt. Krish)
From Christopher, meaning 'bearing Christ inside'.

Kurt
German, meaning 'courageous advice'.

Kurtis
French, meaning 'courtier'.

Kwame
Ghanaian, meaning 'born on Saturday'.

Kyden
English, meaning 'narrow little fire'.

Kylan
(alt. Kyle, Kyleb, Kyler)
Gaelic, meaning 'narrow and straight'.

Kyllion
Irish, meaning 'war'.

Kyree
From Cree, a Canadian tribe.

Kyros
Greek, meaning 'legitimate power'.

L Boys' names

Laban

Hebrew, meaning 'white'.

Lachlan

Gaelic, meaning 'from the land of lakes'.

Lacy

Old French place name.

Lalit

Hindi, meaning 'beautiful'.

Lamar

Old German, meaning 'water'.

Lambert

Scandinavian, meaning 'land brilliant'.

Lambros

Greek, meaning 'brilliant and radiant'.

Lamont

Old Norse, meaning 'law man'.

Lance

French, meaning 'land'.

Lancelot

Variant of Lance, meaning 'land'. The name of one of the knights of the Round Table.

Landen

(alt. Lando, Landon, Langdon)

English, meaning 'long hill'.

L

Landyn
Welsh variant of Landen, meaning 'long hill'.

Lane
(alt. Layne)
English, from the word 'lanel'.

Lannie
(alt. Lanny)
German, meaning 'precious'.

Larkin
Gaelic, meaning 'rough' or 'fierce'.

Laron
French, meaning 'thief'.

Larry
French, meaning 'man from Laurentum'.

Lars
Scandinavian variant of Lawrence, meaning 'man from Laurentum'.

Lasse
Finnish, meaning 'girl'. (Still, ironically, a boy's name.)

Laszlo
Hungarian, meaning 'glorious rule'.

Lathyn
Latin, meaning 'fighter'.

Latif
Arabic, meaning 'gentle'.

Laurel
Latin, meaning 'bay'.

Laurent
French, from Lawrence, meaning 'man from Laurentum'.

Lawrence
Latin, meaning 'man from Laurentum'.

Lazarus
Hebrew, meaning 'God is my help'.

Leandro
Latin, meaning 'lion man'.

L

Lear

German, meaning 'of the meadow'.

Lee

(alt. Leigh)

Old English, meaning 'meadow' or 'valley'.

Leib

German, meaning 'love'.

Leif

Scandinavian, meaning 'heir'.

Leith

From the name of a place in Scotland.

Lennox

(alt. Lenny)

Gaelic, meaning 'with many Elm trees'.

Leo

Latin, meaning 'lion'.

Leon

Latin, meaning 'lion'.

Leonard

Old German, meaning 'lion strength'.

Leopold

German, meaning 'brave people'.

Leroy

French, meaning 'king'.

Lesley

(alt. Les)

Scottish, meaning 'holly garden'.

Lester

English, meaning 'from Leicester'.

Lewis

French, meaning 'renowned fighter'.

Liam

German, meaning 'helmet'.

Lincoln

English, meaning 'lake colony'.

L

Lindsay
Scottish, meaning 'linden tree'.

Linus
Latin, meaning 'lion'.

Lionel
English, meaning 'lion'.

Llewellyn
Welsh, meaning 'like a lion'.

Lloyd
Welsh, meaning 'grey-haired and sacred'.

Logan
Gaelic, meaning 'hollow'.

Lonnie
English, meaning 'lion strength'.

Lorcan
Gaelic, meaning 'little fierce one'.

Louis
(alt. Lou, Louie, Luigi, Luis)
German, meaning 'famous warrior'.

Lucian
(alt. Lucio)
Latin, meaning 'light'.

Ludwig
German, meaning 'famous fighter'.

Luke
(alt. Luc, Luka)
Latin, meaning 'from Lucanus' (in southern Italy).

Lupe
Latin, meaning 'wolf'.

Luther
German, meaning 'soldier of the people'.

Lyle
French, meaning 'the island'.

Lyn
(alt. Lyndon)
Spanish, meaning 'pretty'.

 Boys' names

Mac
(alt. Mack, Mackie)
Scottish, meaning 'son of'.

Macaulay
Scottish, meaning 'son of the phantom'.

Mace
English, meaning 'heavy staff' or 'club'.

Mackenzie
Scottish, meaning 'the fair one'.

Mackland
Scottish, meaning 'land of Mac'.

Macon
French origin, name of towns in France and Georgia.

Macsen
Scottish, meaning 'son of Mac'.

Madden
Irish, meaning 'descendant of the hound'.

Maddox
English, meaning 'good' or 'generous'.

Madison
(alt. Madsen)
Irish, meaning 'son of Madden'.

M

Mads

Shortened form of Madden, meaning 'descendant of the hound'.

Magnus
(alt. Manus)

Latin, meaning 'great'.

Maguire

Gaelic, meaning 'son of the beige one'.

Mahesh

Hindi, meaning 'great ruler'.

Mahir

Arabic, meaning 'skillful'.

Mahlon

Hebrew, meaning 'sickness'.

Mahmoud

Arabic, meaning 'praiseworthy'.

Mahoney

Irish, meaning 'bear'.

Major

English, from the word 'major'.

Makal

From Michael, meaning 'close to God'.

Makani

Hawaiian, meaning 'wind'.

Makis

Hebrew, meaning 'gift from God'.

Mako

Hebrew, meaning 'God is with us'.

Malachi
(alt. Malachy)

Irish, meaning 'messenger of God'.

Malcolm

English, meaning 'Columba's servant'.

Mali

Arabic, meaning 'full and rich'.

Manfred

Old German, meaning 'man of peace'.

M

Manish

English, meaning 'manly'.

Manley

English, meaning 'manly and brave'.

Mannix

Gaelic, meaning 'little monk'.

Manoi
(alt. Manos)

Japanese, meaning 'love springing from intellect'.

Manuel

Hebrew, meaning 'God is with us'.

Manzi

Italian, meaning 'steer'.

Marc
(alt. Marco, Marcos, Marcus, Markel)

French, meaning 'from the god Mars'.

Marcel
(alt. Marcelino, Marcello)

French, meaning 'little warrior'.

Marek

Polish variant of Mark ,meaning 'from the god Mars'.

Mariano

Latin, meaning 'from the god Mars'.

Mario
(alt. Marius)

Latin, meaning 'manly'.

Mark

English, meaning 'from the god Mars'.

Marley
(alt. Marlin)

Old English, meaning 'meadow near the lake'.

Marshall

Old French, meaning 'caretaker of horses'.

Martin

Latin, meaning 'dedicated to Mars'.

Marty

Shortened form of Martin, meaning 'dedicated to Mars'.

M

Marvel

English, from the word 'marvel'.

Marvin

Welsh, meaning 'sea friend'.

Mason

English, from the word mason.

Mathias

(alt. Matthias)

Hebrew, meaning 'gift of God'.

Mathieu

French form of Matthew, meaning 'gift of God'.

Matthew

Hebrew, meaning 'gift of the Lord'.

Maurice

(alt. Mauricio)

Latin, meaning 'dark skinned' or 'Moorish'.

Maverick

American origin, meaning 'non-conformist leader'.

Max

(alt. Maxie, Maxim)

Latin, meaning 'greatest'.

Maximillian

Latin, meaning 'greatest'.

Maximino

Latin, meaning 'little Max'.

Maxwell

Latin, meaning 'Maccus' stream'.

Maynard

Old German, meaning 'brave'.

McArthur

Scottish, meaning 'son of Arthur'.

McCoy

Scottish, meaning 'son of Coy'.

Mearl

English, meaning 'my earl'.

Mederic

French, meaning 'doctor'.

Mekhi

African, meaning 'who is God?'

Mel

Gaelic, meaning 'smooth brow'.

Melbourne

From the city in Australia.

Melchior

Persian, meaning 'king of the city'.

Melton

English, meaning 'town of Mel'.

Melva

Hawaiian, meaning 'plumeria'.

Melville

Scottish, meaning 'town of Mel'.

Melvin

(alt. Melvyn)

English, meaning 'smooth brow'.

Memphis

Greek, meaning 'established and beautiful'. Also the name of a city in the USA.

Mercer

English, from the word 'mercer'.

Merl

French, meaning 'blackbird'.

Merlin

Welsh, meaning 'sea fortress'.

Merrick

Welsh, meaning 'Moorish'.

Merrill

Gaelic, meaning 'shining sea'.

Merritt

English, from the word 'merit'.

Merton

Old English, meaning 'town by the lake'.

Meyer

Hebrew, meaning 'bright farmer'.

Michael

Hebrew, meaning 'resembles God'. One of the archangels.

Michalis

Greek form of Michael, meaning 'resembles God'.

Michel

French form of Michael, meaning 'resembles God'.

Michelangelo

Italian, meaning 'Michael's angel'. Name of the famous painter.

Michele

Italian form of Michael, meaning 'resembles God'.

Mickey

Variant of Michael meaning 'resembles God'.

Miguel

Spanish form of Michael meaning 'resembles God'.

Mike

Shortened form of Michael meaning 'resembles God'.

Miklos

Greek form of Michael meaning 'resembles God'.

Milan

From the name of the Italian city.

Miles

(alt. Milo, Milos, Myles)
English, from the word 'miles'.

Milton

English, meaning 'miller's town'. Also the name of the poet.

Miro

Slavic, meaning 'peace'.

Misha

Russian, meaning 'who is like God'.

Mitch

Shortened form of Mitchell, meaning 'who is like God'.

Mitchell

English, meaning 'who is like God'.

M

Football players

Bobby (Charlton/Moore)
David (Beckham)
Gary (Lineker/Neville)
Geoff (Hurst)
Kenny (Dalglish)
Kevin (Keegan)
Michael (Owen)
Ryan (Giggs)
Stanley (Matthews)

Modesto

Italian, meaning 'modest'.

Moe

Hebrew, meaning 'God's helmet'.

Mohamed

(alt. Mohammad, Mohamet, Mohammed)

Arabic, meaning 'praiseworthy'.

Monroe

Gaelic, meaning 'mouth of the river Rotha'.

Monserrate

Latin, meaning 'jagged mountain'.

Montague

French, meaning 'pointed hill'.

Montana

Latin, meaning 'mountain'. Also a state in the USA.

Monte

Italian, meaning 'mountain'.

Montgomery

Variant of Montague, meaning 'pointed hill'.

Monty

Shortened form of Montague, meaning 'pointed hill'.

Moody

English, from the word 'moody'.

Mordecai

Hebrew, meaning 'little man'.

Morgan

Welsh, meaning 'circling sea'.

M

Moritz
Latin, meaning 'dark skinned and Moorish'.

Morpheus
Greek, meaning 'shape'.

Morris
Welsh, meaning 'dark skinned and Moorish'.

Morrison
English, meaning 'son of Morris'.

Mortimer
French, meaning 'dead sea'.

Morton
Old English, meaning 'moor town'.

Moses
(alt. Moshe, Moshon)
Hebrew, meaning 'saviour'. In the Bible Moses receives the Ten Commandments from God.

Moss
English, from the word 'moss'.

Mungo
Gaelic, meaning 'most dear'.

Murl
French, meaning 'blackbird'.

Murphy
Irish, meaning 'sea warrior'.

Murray
Gaelic, meaning 'lord and master'.

Mustafa
Arabic, meaning 'chosen'.

Myron
Greek, meaning 'myrrh'.

 Boys' names

Najee

Arabic, meaning 'dear companion'.

Nakia

Arabic, meaning 'pure'.

Nakul

Indian, meaning 'mongoose'.

Naphtali

Hebrew, meaning 'wrestling'.

Napoleon

Italian origin, meaning 'man from Naples'. Name of the French general who became Emperor of France.

Narciso

Latin, from the myth of Narcissus, famous for drowning after gazing at his own reflection.

Nash

English, meaning 'at the ash tree'.

Nasir

Arabic, meaning 'helper'.

Nate

Hebrew, meaning 'God has given'.

Nathan

(alt. Nathaniel)

Hebrew, meaning 'God has given'.

Popular song names

Alexander (*Alexander's Ragtime Band*, Irving Berlin)
Daniel (*Daniel*, Elton John)
Frankie (*Frankie*, Sister Sledge)
Jack (*Jumpin' Jack Flash*, The Rolling Stones)
James (*James Dean*, The Eagles)
Johnny (*Johnny B. Goode*, Chuck Berry)
Kenneth (*What's the Frequency, Kenneth?*, REM)
Leroy (*Bad, Bad Leroy Brown*, Jim Croce)
Mack (*Mack The Knife*, Bobby Darin)
Oliver (*Oliver's Army*, Elvis Costello)

Naveen
Indian, meaning 'new'.

Neal
Irish, meaning 'champion'.

Ned
Nickname for Edward, meaning 'wealthy guard'.

Neftali
Hebrew, meaning 'struggling'.

Nehemiah
Hebrew, meaning 'comforter'.

Neil
(alt. Niall)
Irish, meaning 'champion'.

Neilson
Irish, meaning 'son of Neil'.

Nelson
Variant of Neil, meaning 'champion'

Nemo
Latin, meaning 'nobody'.

Neo
Latin, meaning 'new'.

N

Nephi
Greek, meaning 'cloud'.

Nessim
Arabic, meaning 'breeze'.

Nestor
Greek, meaning 'traveller'.

Neville
Old French, meaning 'new village'.

Newton
English, meaning 'new town'.

Nicholas
(alt. Niklas)
Greek, meaning 'victorious'.

Nick
(alt. Niko, Nikos)
Shortened form of Nicholas, meaning 'victorious'.

Nico
Variant of Nicholas, meaning 'victorious'.

Nigel
Gaelic, meaning 'champion'.

Nikhil
Hindi, meaning 'whole' or 'entire'.

Nikita
Greek, meaning 'unconquered'.

Nikolai
Russian variant of Nicholas, meaning 'victorious'.

Nimrod
Hebrew, meaning 'we will rebel'.

Nissim
Hebrew, meaning 'wonderful things'.

Noah
Hebrew, meaning 'peaceful'.

Noel
French, meaning 'Christmas'.

Nolan
Gaelic, meaning 'champion'.

N

Norbert

Old German, meaning 'Northern brightness'.

Norman

Old German, meaning 'Northerner'.

Normand

French, meaning 'from Normandy'.

Norris

Old French, meaning 'Northerner'.

Norton

English, meaning 'Northern town'.

Norval

French, meaning 'Northern town'.

Norwood

English, meaning 'Northern forest'.

Nova

Latin, meaning 'new'.

Nuno

Latin, meaning 'ninth'.

Nunzio

Italian, meaning 'messenger'.

Names of Gods

Anubis (Death: Egyptian)
Apollo (Sun: Roman)
Brahma (Creation: Indian)
Eros (Love: Greek)
Hypnos (Sleep: Greek)
Mars (War: Roman)
Neptune (Sea: Roman)
Ra (Sun: Egyptian)
Shiva (Destruction: Indian)
Vishnu (Preservation: Indian)

Boys' names

Oakley

English, meaning 'from the oak meadow'.

Obadiah

Biblical, meaning 'God's worker'.

Obama

African, meaning 'crooked'. Made famous by the American President Barack Obama.

Obed

Hebrew, meaning 'servant of God'.

Spelling options

F vs PH (Josef or Joseph)
I vs Y (Henri or Henry)
J vs G (Jorge or George)
N vs HN (Jon or John)
QUE vs CK (Frederique or Frederick)
T vs TH (Antony or Anthony)

O

Oberon

Old German, meaning 'royal bear'.

Obie

Shortened form of Oberon, meaning 'royal bear'.

Octave

(alt. Octavian, Octavio)

Latin, meaning 'eight'.

Oda

(alt. Odell, Odie, Odis)

Hebrew, meaning 'praise God'.

Ogden

Old English, meaning 'oak valley'.

Oisin

From the Irish poet.

Ola

Norse, meaning 'precious'.

Olaf

(alt. Olan)

Old Norse, meaning 'ancestor'.

Oleander

Hawaiian, meaning 'joyous'.

Oleg

(alt. Olen)

Russian, meaning 'holy'.

Olin

Russian, meaning 'rock'.

Oliver

Latin, meaning 'olive tree'.

Olivier

French form of Oliver, meaning 'olive tree'.

Ollie

Shortened form of Oliver, meaning 'olive tree'.

Omar

(alt. Omari, Omarion)

Arabic, meaning 'speaker'.

Ora

Latin, meaning 'hour'.

O

Oran
(alt. Oren, Orrin)
Gaelic, meaning 'light and pale'.

Orange
English, from the word 'orange'.

Orion
From the Greek hunter.

Orlando
(alt. Orlo)
Old German, meaning 'old land'. Name of a city in the USA.

Orpheus
Greek, meaning 'beautiful voice'.

Orson
Latin, meaning 'bear'.

Orville
Old French, meaning 'gold town'.

Osaka
From the Japanese city.

Osborne
Norse, meaning 'bear god'.

Oscar
Old English, meaning 'spear of the Gods'.

Oswald
German, meaning 'God's power'.

Foreign alternatives
David – Dafydd, Davin
John – Jean, Jose, Juan
Michael – Miguel, Mikhail
Peter – Pedro, Pierre, Pieter
Richard – Ricardo

O

Otha
(alt. Otho)
German, meaning 'wealth'.

Othello
From the Shakespearean character.

Otis
German, meaning 'wealth'.

Otten
English, meaning 'otter-like'.

Otto
Italian, meaning 'eight'.

Owain
Welsh, meaning 'youth'.

Owen
Welsh, meaning 'well born and noble'.

Oz
Hebrew, meaning 'strength'.

Popular Asian names for boys and girls

Bao
Cái
Huang
Jiro
Kei
Ming
Miyoko
Shen
Tai
Yoko

P

Boys' names

Pablo
Spanish, meaning 'little'.

Padma
Indian, meaning 'lotus'.

Padraig
Irish, meaning 'noble'.

Panos
Greek, meaning 'all holy'.

Paolo
Italian, meaning 'little'.

Paresh
Indian, meaning 'supreme standard'.

Pascal
Latin, meaning 'Easter child'.

Pat
Shortened form of Patrick, meaning 'noble'.

Patrice
Variant of Patrick, meaning 'noble'.

Patrick
Irish, meaning 'noble'.

Patten
English, meaning 'noble'.

Paul
Biblical, meaning 'small'.

P

Pavel

Latin, meaning 'small'.

Pax

Latin, meaning 'peace'.

Paxton

English, meaning 'town of peace'.

Payne

Latin, meaning 'peasant'.

Payton

Latin, meaning 'peasant's town'.

Pedro

Spanish form of Peter, meaning 'rock'.

Penn

English, meaning 'hill'.

Percival

French, meaning 'pierce the valley'.

Percy

Shortened form of Percival, meaning 'pierce the valley'.

Perez

Hebrew, meaning 'breach'.

Pericles

Greek, meaning 'far-famed'.

Perrin

Greek, meaning 'rock'.

Perry

English, meaning 'rock'.

Pervis

English, meaning 'purveyor'.

Pete

Shortened form of Peter, meaning 'rock'.

Peter

English, meaning 'rock'.

Petros

Spanish form of Peter, meaning 'rock'.

Peyton

Old English, meaning 'fighting man's estate'.

P

Phil

Shortened form of Philip, meaning 'lover of horses'.

Philip

Greek, meaning 'lover of horses'.

Philo

Greek, meaning 'love'.

Phineas

(alt. Pinchas)

Hebrew, meaning 'oracle'.

Phoenix

Greek, meaning 'dark red'.

Pierre

French form of Peter, meaning 'stone'.

Piers

Greek form of Peter, meaning 'rock'.

Pierson

Variant of Peirce, meaning 'son of Piers'.

Pip

Greek, meaning 'lover of horses'.

Placido

Latin, meaning 'placid'.

Pradeep

Hindi, meaning 'light'.

Pranav

Hindi, meaning 'spiritual leader'.

Presley

Old English, meaning 'priest's meadow'.

Preston

Old English, meaning 'priest's town'.

No-nickname names

Alex
Jude
Keith
Otto
Owen
Toby

P

Primo

Italian, meaning 'first'.

Primus

Latin, meaning 'first'.

Prince

English, from the word 'prince'.

Prospero

Latin, meaning 'prosperous'.

Pryor

English, meaning 'first'.

Ptolemy

Greek, meaning 'aggressive' or 'warlike'.

Popular Australian names for boys and girls

Adelaide
Brad
Darwin
Evonne
Griffith
Hobart
Lorrae
Narelle
Raelene
Tallara

Boys' names

Quabil
Arabic, meaning 'able'.

Quadim
Arabic, meaning 'able'.

Quadir
Arabic, meaning 'powerful'.

Quaid
Irish, meaning 'fourth'.

Quemby
Norse, meaning 'from the woman's estate'.

Quentin
(alt. Quinten, Quintin, Quinton, Quintus)
Latin, meaning 'fifth'.

Quillan
Gaelic, meaning 'sword'.

Quillon
Gaelic, meaning 'club'.

Quincy
Old French, meaning 'estate of the fifth son'.

Quinlan
Gaelic, meaning 'fit, shapely and strong'.

Quinn
Gaelic, meaning 'counsel'.

'Powerful' names

Derek
Hercules
Michio
Oswald
Oz
Roderick
Thor

R Boys' names

Radames
Slavic, meaning 'famous joy'.

Raekwon
Hebrew, meaning 'God has healed'.

Rafael
(alt. Rafe, Rafer, Raffi, Raphael)
Hebrew, meaning 'God has healed'. One of the archangels.

Ragnar
Old Norse, meaning 'judgement warrior'.

Raheem
Arabic, meaning 'merciful and kind'.

Rahm
Hebrew, meaning 'pleasing'.

Rahul
(alt. Raoul, Raul)
Indian, meaning 'efficient'.

Raiden
(alt. Rainen)
From the Japanese god of thunder.

Raj
Indian, meaning 'king'.

Rajesh
(alt. Ramesh)
Indian, meaning 'ruler of kings'.

Raleigh
Old English, meaning 'deer's meadow'.

Ralph
Old English, meaning 'wolf'.

R

Ram

English, from the word 'ram'.

Ramiro

Germanic, meaning 'powerful in battle'.

Ramsey
(alt. Ramsay)

Old English, meaning 'wild garlic island'.

Randall
(alt. Randolph)

Old German, meaning 'wolf shield'.

Randy

Variant of Randall, meaning 'wolf shield'. In modern English, randy can also mean amorous.

Raniel

English, meaning 'God is my happiness'.

Ranjit

Indian, meaning 'influenced by charm'.

Rannoch

Gaelic, meaning 'fern'.

Rashad

Arabic, meaning 'good judgment'.

Rasheed
(alt. Rashid)

Indian, meaning 'rightly guided'.

Rasmus

Greek, meaning 'beloved'.

Raven

English, from the word 'raven'.

Ravi

French, meaning 'delighted'.

Ray

English, from the word 'ray'.

Raymond
(alt. Rayner)

English, meaning 'advisor'.

Raz

Israeli, meaning 'secret' or 'mystery'.

Reagan

Irish, meaning 'little king'.

R

Reggie

Latin, meaning 'queen'.

Reginald

Latin, meaning 'regal'.

Regis

Shortened form of Reginald, meaning 'regal'.

Reid

Old English, meaning 'by the reeds'.

Reilly

English, meaning courageous.

Remus

Latin, meaning 'swift'.

Rémy

French, meaning 'from Rheims'.

Ren

Shortened form of Reginald, meaning 'regal'.

Renato

Latin, meaning 'rebirth'.

Rene

French, meaning 'rebirth'.

Reno

Latin, meaning 'renewed'.

Reuben

Spanish, meaning 'a son'.

Reuel

Hebrew, meaning 'friend of God'.

Rex

Latin, meaning 'king'.

Rey

Spanish, meaning 'king'.

Reynold

Latin, meaning 'king's advisor'.

Rhodes

German, meaning 'where the roses grow'. Also the name of the Greek town.

Rhodri

Welsh, meaning 'ruler of the circle'.

Rhys

Welsh, meaning 'enthusiasm'.

Richard

Old German, meaning 'powerful leader'.

Richie

Shortened form of Richard, meaning 'powerful leader'.

Rick

Shortened form of Richard, meaning 'powerful leader'.

Ricki

Shortened form of Richard, meaning 'powerful leader'.

Ricky

Shortened form of Richard, meaning 'powerful leader'.

Ridley

English, meaning 'cleared wood'.

Rigby

English, from the place in Lancashire.

Ringo

English, meaning 'ring'.

Rio

Spanish, meaning 'river'.

Riordan

Gaelic, meaning 'bard'.

Rishi

Variant of Richard, meaning 'powerful leader'.

Ritchie

Shortened form of Richard, meaning 'powerful leader'.

Roald

Scandinavian, meaning 'ruler'.

Rob

Shortened form of Robert, meaning 'bright fame'.

Robbie

Shortened form of Robert, meaning 'bright fame'.

Robert

Old German, meaning 'bright fame'.

Roberto

Variant of Robert, meaning 'bright fame'.

R

Robin

English, from the word 'robin'.

Robinson

English, meaning 'son of Robin'.

Rocco

(alt. Rocky)

Italian, meaning 'rest'.

Rod

Short for both Rhodri and Rodney.

Roderick

German, meaning 'famous power'.

Rodney

Old German, meaning 'island near the clearing'.

Rodrigo

Spanish form of Roderick, meaning 'famous power'.

Roger

Old German, meaning 'spear man'.

Roland

Old German, meaning 'renowned land'.

Rolf

Old German, meaning 'wolf'.

Rollie

(alt. Rollo)

Old German, meaning 'renowned land'.

Roman

Latin, meaning 'from Rome'.

Romeo

Latin, meaning 'pilgrim to Rome'. Made famous by Shakespeare's play.

Ron

(alt. Ronnie)

Shortened form of Ronald, meaning 'mountain of strength'.

Ronald

Norse, meaning 'mountain of strength'.

Ronan

Gaelic, meaning 'little seal'.

R

Rory

English, meaning 'red king'.

Ross

(alt. Russ)

Scottish, meaning 'cape'.

Rowan

(alt. Roan)

Gaelic, meaning 'little red one'. Also reference to the rowan tree.

Roy

Gaelic, meaning 'red'.

Ruben

Hebrew, meaning 'son'.

Rudolph

Old German, meaning 'famous wolf'.

Rudy

Shortened form of Rudolph, meaning 'famous wolf'.

Rufus

Latin, meaning 'red-haired'.

Rupert

Variant of Robert, meaning 'bright fame'.

Russell

Old French, meaning 'little red one'.

Rusty

English, meaning 'ruddy'.

Ryan

Gaelic, meaning 'little king'.

Ryder

English, meaning 'horseman'.

Rye

English, from the word 'rye'.

Ryker

From Richard, meaning 'powerful leader'.

Rylan

English, meaning 'land where rye is grown'.

Ryley

Old English, meaning 'rye clearing'.

S Boys' names

Saber
French, meaning 'sword'.

Sagar
African, meaning 'ruler of the water'.

Sage
English, meaning 'wise'.

Sakari
Native American, meaning 'sweet'.

Salim
Arabic, meaning 'secure'.

Salvador
Spanish, meaning 'saviour'.

Salvatore
Italian, meaning 'saviour'.

Sam
(alt. Sama, Sammie, Sammy)
Hebrew, meaning 'God is heard'.

Samir
Arabic, meaning 'pleasant companion'.

Spring names

Alvern
Jarek
Kell
Marcus
Tamiko

S

Samson

Hebrew, meaning 'son of Sam'.

Samuel

Hebrew, meaning 'God is heard'.

Sandeep

Indian, meaning 'lighting the way'.

Sandro

Shortened form of Alessandro, meaning 'defending men'.

Sandy

Shortened form of Alexander, meaning 'defending men'.

Sanjay

Indian, meaning 'victory'.

Santiago

Spanish, meaning 'Saint James'.

Santino

Spanish, meaning 'little Saint James'.

Santo

(alt. Santos)

Latin, meaning 'Saint'.

Sascha

Shortened Russian form of Alexander, meaning 'defending men'.

Scott

(alt. Scottie)

English, meaning 'from Scotland'.

Seamus

Irish variant of James, meaning 'he who supplants'.

Sean

(alt. Shaun)

Variant of John, meaning 'God is gracious'.

Sebastian

Greek, meaning 'revered'.

Sébastien

French form of Sebastian, meaning 'revered'.

Sergio

Latin, meaning 'servant'.

Seth

Hebrew, meaning 'appointed'.

S

Severus

Latin, meaning 'severe'.

Seymour

From the place name in northern France.

Shane

Variant of Sean, meaning 'God is gracious'.

Sharif

Arabic, meaning 'honoured'.

Shea

Gaelic, meaning 'admirable'.

Shelby

Norse, meaning 'willow'.

Sherlock

English, meaning 'fair haired'.

Sherman

Old English, meaning 'shear man'.

Shmuel

Hebrew, meaning 'his name is God'.

Shola

Arabic, meaning 'energetic'.

Sid

Shortened form of Sidney, meaning 'wide meadow'.

Sidney

English, meaning 'wide meadow'.

Sigmund

Old German, meaning 'victorious hand'.

Silvanus
(alt. Silvio)

Latin, meaning 'woods'.

Sim

Shortened form of Simba, meaning 'lion'.

Summer names

Augustus
Balder
Leo
Sky
Somers

175

S

Simba
Arabic, meaning 'lion'.

Simon
(alt. *Simeon*)
Hebrew, meaning 'to hear'.

Sinbad
Literary merchant adventurer.

Sindri
Norse dwarf.

Sipho
African, meaning 'the unknown one'.

Sire
English, from the word 'sire'.

Sirius
Hebrew, meaning 'brightest star'.

Skipper
English, meaning 'ship captain'.

Socrates
Greek philosopher.

Solomon
Hebrew, meaning 'peace'.

Sonny
American English, meaning 'son'.

Soren
Scandinavian variant of Severus, meaning 'brightest star'.

Spencer
English, meaning 'dispenser'.

Spike
English, from the word 'spike'.

Stan
Shortened form of Stanley, meaning 'stony meadow'.

Stanford
English, meaning 'stone ford'.

Stanley
English, meaning 'stony meadow'.

Stavros
Greek, meaning 'crowned'.

Stellan
Latin, meaning 'starred'.

S

Steno
German, meaning 'stone'.

Stephen
(alt. Stefan, Stefano, Steffan)
English, meaning 'crowned'.

Steven
(alt. Steve, Stevie)
English, meaning 'crowned'.

Stewart
English, meaning 'steward'.

Stoney
English, meaning 'stone like'.

Storm
English, from the word 'storm'.

Stuart
English, meaning 'steward'.

Sven
Norse, meaning 'boy'.

Sydney
English, meaning 'wide meadow'.

Syed
Arabic, meaning 'lucky'.

Sylvester
Latin, meaning 'wooded'.

Autumn names

Aki
Akiko
Demitrius
George
Goren

T

Boys' names

Tacitus

From the Roman historian.

Tad

English, from the word 'tadpole'.

Taj

Indian, meaning 'crown'.

Takashi

Japanese, meaning 'praiseworthy'.

Takoda

Sioux, meaning 'friend to everyone'.

Talbot

(alt. Tal)

Aristocratic English name.

Tamir

Arabic, meaning 'tall and wealthy'.

Taras

(alt. Tarez)

Scottish, meaning 'crag'.

Tarek

Arabic, meaning 'evening caller'.

Tarian

Welsh, meaning 'silver'.

T

Tariq

Arabic, meaning 'morning star'.

Tarquin

From the Roman clan name.

Tarun

Hindi, meaning 'young'.

Tatanka

Hebrew, meaning 'bull'.

Tate

English, meaning 'cheerful'.

Taurean

English, meaning 'bull like'.

Tavares

English, meaning 'descendant of the hermit'.

Tave

(alt. Tavian, Tavis, Tavish)
From Octave, meaning 'eight'.

Taylor

English, meaning 'tailor'.

Ted

(alt. Teddy)
English, from Edward, meaning 'wealthy'.

Terence

(alt. Terrill, Terry)
English, meaning 'tender'.

Tex

English, meaning 'Texan'.

Thane

(alt. Thayer)
Scottish, meaning 'landholder'.

Thelonius

Latin, meaning 'ruler of the people'.

Theo

Shortened form of Theodore, meaning 'God's gift'.

Theodore

Greek, meaning 'God's gift'.

Theophile

Latin, meaning 'God's love'.

T

Theron

Greek, meaning 'hunter'.

Thierry

French variant of Terence, meaning 'tender'.

Thomas

Aramaic, meaning 'twin'.

Thomsen

English, meaning 'son of Thomas'.

Thor

Norse, meaning 'thunder'.

Tiago

From Santiago, meaning 'Saint James'.

Tiberius

English, meaning 'from the river Tiber'.

Tibor

Latin, from river Tiber.

Tiernan

Gaelic, meaning 'lord'.

Tilden

(alt. Till)

English, meaning 'fertile valley'.

Tim

(alt. Timmie, Timon)

Shortened form of Timothy, meaning 'God's honour'.

Timothy

Greek, meaning 'God's honour'.

Tito

(alt. Titus, Tizian)

Latin, meaning 'defender'.

Tobias

(alt. Toby)

Hebrew, meaning 'God is good'.

Tod

(alt. Todd)

English, meaning 'fox'.

Tom

(alt. Tomlin, Tommy)

Hebrew, meaning 'twin'.

Tonneau

French, meaning 'barrel'.

T

Tony
Shortened form of Anthony, from the old Roman family name.

Torey
Norse, meaning 'Thor'.

Torin
Gaelic, meaning 'chief'.

Torquil
Gaelic, meaning 'helmet'.

Toshi
Japanese, meaning 'reflection'.

Travis
French, meaning 'crossover'.

Trevor
Welsh origin, meaning 'great settlement'.

Trey
(alt. Tyree)
French, meaning 'very'.

Tristan
(alt. Tristram)
From the Celtic hero.

Troy
Gaelic, meaning 'descended from the soldier'.

Tudor
Variant of Theodore, 'God's gift'.

Tyler
English, meaning 'tile maker'.

Tyrell
French, meaning 'puller'.

Tyrone
Gaelic, meaning 'Owen's county'.

Tyson
English, meaning 'son of Tyrone'.

Winter names

Aquilo
Caldwell
Jack
Mistral
Rain

 Boys' names

Uberto
(alt. Umberto)
From the Italian royal name.

Udo
German, meaning 'power of the wolf'.

Ugo
Italian form of Hugo, meaning 'mind and heart'.

Ulf
German, meaning 'wolf'.

Ulrich
German, meaning 'noble ruler'.

Ultan
Irish, meaning 'from Ulster'.

Ulysses
Greek, meaning 'wrathful'. Made famous by the mythological voyager.

Upton
English, meaning 'high town'.

Urho
Finnish, meaning 'brave'.

Uri
(alt. Uriah, Urias)
Hebrew, meaning 'my light'.

Uriel
Hebrew, meaning 'angel of light'. One of the archangels.

U

Usher

English, from the word 'usher'.
Made famous by American
R&B star.

Uzi

Hebrew, meaning 'my strength'.

Uzzi

(alt. Uzziah)

Hebrew, meaning 'my power'.

Christmas names

Casper
Celyn
Christian
Gabriel
Jesus
Joseph
Nicholas
Noel

Boys' names

Vadim
Russian, meaning 'scandal maker'.

Valdemar
German, meaning 'renowned leader'.

Valente
Latin, meaning 'valiant'.

Valentin
(alt. Val)
French, meaning 'valentine'.

Valentine
English, from the word 'valentine'.

Valentino
Italian, meaning 'valentine'.

Valerio
Italian, meaning 'valiant'.

Van
Dutch, meaning 'son of'.

Vance
English, meaning 'marshland'.

Vangelis
Greek, meaning 'good news'.

Varun
Hindi, meaning 'water god'.

Vasilis
Greek, meaning 'kingly'.

Vaughan
Welsh, meaning 'little'.

V

Vernell

French, meaning 'green and flourishing'.

Verner

German, meaning 'army defender'.

Vernon
(alt. Vernie)

French, meaning 'alder grove'.

Versilius

Latin, meaning 'flier'.

Vester

Latin, meaning 'wooded'.

Victor

Latin, meaning 'champion'.

Vidal
(alt. Vidar)

Spanish, meaning 'life giving'.

Vijay

Hindi, meaning 'conquering'.

Vikram

Hindi, meaning 'sun'.

Viktor

Latin, meaning 'victory'.

Ville

French, meaning 'town'.

Vincent
(alt. Vince)

English, meaning 'victorious'.

Virgil

From the Latin poet.

Vito

Spanish, meaning 'life'.

Vittorio

Italian, meaning 'victory'.

Vitus

Latin, meaning 'life'.

Vivian

Latin, meaning 'lively'.

Vladimir

Slavic, meaning 'prince'.

Volker

German, meaning 'defender of the people'.

Von

Norse, meaning 'hope'.

W

Boys' names

Wade

English, meaning 'to move forward' or 'to go'.

Waldemar

German, meaning 'famous ruler'.

Walden

English, meaning 'valley of the Britons'.

Waldo

Old German, meaning 'rule'.

Walker

English, meaning 'a fuller'.

Wallace

English, meaning 'foreigner' or 'stranger'.

Wally

German, meaning 'ruler of the army'.

Walter

(alt. Walt)

German, meaning 'ruler of the army'.

Ward

English, meaning 'guardian'.

Wardell

Old English, meaning 'watchman's hill'.

Warner

German, meaning 'army guard'.

Warren

German, meaning 'guard' or 'the game park'.

Washington

English, meaning 'clever' or 'clever man's settlement'.

Wassily

Greek, meaning 'royal' or 'kingly'.

Watson

English, meaning 'son' or 'son of Walter'.

Waverley
(alt. Waverly)

English, meaning 'quaking aspen'.

Waylon

English, meaning 'land by the road'.

Wayne

English, meaning 'a cartwright'.

Webster

English, meaning 'weaver'.

Weldon

English, meaning 'from the hill of well' or 'hill with a well'.

Wendell
(alt. Wendel)

German, meaning 'a wend'.

Werner

German, meaning 'army guard'.

Weston

English, meaning 'from the west town'.

Wheeler

English, meaning 'wheel maker'.

Whitley

English, meaning 'white wood'.

Whitman

Old English, meaning 'white man'.

Whitney

Old English, meaning 'white island'.

Wilber

(alt. Wilbur)

Old German, meaning 'bright will'.

Wiley

Old English, meaning 'beguiling' or 'enchanting'.

Wilford

Old English, meaning 'the ford by the willows'.

Wilfredo

(alt. Wilfred, Wilfrid)

English, meaning 'to will peace'.

Wilhelm

German, meaning 'strong-willed warrior'.

Wilkes

(alt. Wilkie)

Old English, meaning 'strong-willed protector' or 'strong and resolute protector'.

William

(alt. Will, Willie)

English (Teutonic), meaning 'strong protector' or 'strong-willed warrior'.

Willis

English, meaning 'server of Will'.

Willoughby

Old Norse and Old English, meaning 'from the farm by the trees'.

Wilmer

English (Teutonic), meaning 'famously resolute'.

Wilmot

English, meaning 'resolute mind'.

Wilson

English, meaning 'son of William'.

Wilton

Old Norse and English, meaning 'from the farm by the brook' or 'from the farm by the streams'.

Windell
(alt. Wendell)

German, meaning 'wanderer' or 'seeker'.

Windsor

Old English, meaning 'river bank' or 'landing place'.

Winfield

English, meaning 'from the field of Wina'.

Winslow

Old English, meaning 'victory on the hill'.

Winter

Old English, meaning 'to be born in the winter'.

Winthrop

Old English, meaning 'village of friends'.

Winton

Old English, meaning 'a friend's farm'.

Wirrin

Aboriginal, meaning 'a tea tree'.

Food-inspired names

Ale
Basil
Berry
Cane
Rye
Shad
Tamir

Wistan

Old English, meaning 'battle stone' or 'mark of the battle'.

Wittan

Old English, meaning 'farm in the woods' or 'farm by the woods'.

Wolf
(alt. Wolfe)

English, meaning 'strong as a wolf'.

Wolfgang

Teutonic, meaning 'the path of wolves'.

Wolfrom

Teutonic, meaning 'raven wolf'.

Wolter

Dutch, a form of Walter meaning 'ruler of the army'.

Woodburn

Old English, meaning 'a stream in the woods'.

Woodrow

English, meaning 'from the row of houses by the wood'.

Woodward

English, meaning 'guardian of the forest'.

Woody

American, meaning 'path in the woods'.

Worcester

Old English, meaning 'from a Roman site'.

Worth

American, meaning 'worth much' or 'wealthy place' or 'wealth and riches'.

Wren

Old English, meaning 'tiny bird'.

Wright

Old English, meaning 'to be a craftsman' or 'from a carpenter'.

Wyatt

Teutonic, meaning 'from wood' or 'from the wide water'.

Wynn

(alt. Wyn)

Welsh, meaning 'very blessed' or 'the fair blessed one'.

Popular English names for boys and girls

Ada
Darren
Dudley
Faith
Garrett
Julian
Lana
Lauren
Posy
Rodney

Boys' names

Xadrian

American, a combination of X and Adrian, meaning 'from Hadria'.

Xander

Greek, meaning 'defender of the people'.

Xanthus

Greek, meaning 'golden-haired'.

Xavier

Latin, meaning 'to the new house'.

Xenon

Greek, meaning 'the guest'.

Xerxes

Persian, meaning 'ruler of the people' or 'respected king'.

Xylander

Greek, meaning 'man of the forest'.

Bird names

Drake
Efron
Gannet
Jay
Robin

 Boys' names

Yaal

Hebrew, meaning 'ascending' or 'one to ascend'.

Yadid

Hebrew, meaning 'the beloved one'.

Yadon

Hebrew, meaning 'against judgment'.

Yahir

Spanish, meaning 'handsome one'.

Yakiya

Hebrew, meaning 'pure' or 'bright'.

Yair

Hebrew, meaning 'the enlightening one' or 'illuminating'.

Yanis
(alt. Yannis)

Greek, a form of John meaning 'gift of God'.

Yarden

Hebrew, meaning 'to flow downward'.

Ye

Chinese, meaning 'bright one' or 'light'.

Yehuda

Hebrew, meaning 'to praise and exalt'.

Yered

Hebrew, a form of Jared, meaning 'descending'.

Yerik

Russian, meaning 'God-appointed one'.

Yervant

Armenian, meaning 'King of people'.

Yitzak

(alt. Yitzaak)

Hebrew, meaning 'laughter' or 'one who laughs'.

Ynyr

Welsh, meaning 'to honour'.

Yobachi

African, meaning 'one who prays to God' or 'prayed to God'.

Yogi

Japanese, meaning 'one who practises yoga' or 'from yoga'.

Yona

Native American, meaning 'bear'; Hebrew, meaning 'dove'.

York

Celtic, meaning 'yew tree' or 'from the farm of the yew tree'.

Yosef

Hebrew, meaning 'added by God' or 'God shall add'.

Yuri

Aboriginal, meaning 'to hear'; Japanese, meaning 'one to listen'; Russian, a form of George meaning 'farmer'.

Yves

French, meaning 'miniature archer' or 'small archer'.

Z Boys' names

Zachariah

(alt. Zac, Zach, Zachary)

Hebrew, meaning 'remembered by the Lord' or 'God has remembered'.

Zad

Persian, meaning 'my son'.

Zadok

Hebrew, meaning 'righteous one'.

Zador

Hungarian, meaning 'violent demeanour'.

Zafar

Arabic, meaning 'triumphant'.

Zaid

African, meaning 'increase the growth' or 'growth'.

Zaide

Yiddish, meaning 'the elder ones'.

Zain

(alt. Zane)

Arabic, meaning 'the handsome son'.

Zaire

African, meaning 'river from Zaire'.

Zander

Greek, meaning 'defender of my people'.

Z

Zarek

Persian, meaning 'God protect our King'.

Names from nature

Ash
Condor
Flint
River
Tiger

part three

Girls' Names

Girls' names

A'mari

Variation on the Swahili or Muslim name Amira, meaning 'princess'.

Aanya

Variation on the Russian name Anya, meaning 'favour' or 'grace'. Also of Sanskrit origin, meaning 'the inexhaustible'.

Aaryanna

Derivative of the Latin name Ariadne and the Greek Ariadne, both meaning 'the very holy one'.

Abby
(alt. Abbey, Abbie)

Form of Abigail, meaning 'my father's joy' in Hebrew.

Abigail
(alt. Abagail, Abbiegayle, Abbigail, Abigale, Abigayle)

Hebrew, meaning 'my father's joy'.

Abilene
(alt. Abilee)

Variation of Abelena. Latin and Spanish for 'hazelnut'.

Abra

Female variation of Abraham. Also of Sanskrit origin, meaning 'clouds'.

Abril

Spanish for the month of April. Also of Latin origin, meaning 'open'.

Acacia

A species of flowering trees and shrubs and derived from the Greek for 'point' or 'thorn'.

Acadia

An offshoot of the Greek word arcadia meaning 'paradise'. Originally, a French colony in Canada.

Ada

(alt. Adair)

Hebrew, meaning 'adornment'.

Adalee

German, meaning 'noble'.

Adalia

'God is my refuge' in Hebrew.

Addie

(alt. Addy, Adi)

Abbreviated form of Addison, Adelaide, Adele and Adeline.

Addison

(alt. Addisyn, Addyson)

English, meaning 'son of Adam'.

Movie inspirations

Beatrix (*Kill Bill*)
Cadey (*Mean Girls*)
Cher (*Clueless*)
Dori (*Finding Nemo*)
Loretta (*The Life of Brian*)
Marla (*Fight Club*)
Paikea (*Whale Rider*)
Ripley (*Aliens*)
Summer (*School of Rock*)
Trinity (*The Matrix*)

A

Adelaide

(alt. Adelaida)

German, popular after the rule of William IV and Queen Adelaide of England in the 19th century.

Adele

(alt. Adela, Adelia, Adell, Adella, Adelle)

German, meaning 'noble' or 'nobility'.

Adeline

(alt. Adalyn, Adalynn, Adelina, Adelyn)

Variant of Adelaide, meaning 'nobility'.

Aden

(alt. Addien)

Hebrew for 'decoration'.

Aderyn

Welsh for 'bird'.

Adesina

Nigerian for 'she paves the way'. Usually given to a first-born daughter.

Adia

Variant of Ada, meaning 'decoration'.

Adina

(alt. Adena)

Hebrew, meaning 'high hopes' or 'precious'.

Adira

Hebrew for 'noble' or 'powerful'. Also the north Italian city.

Adrian

Italian, from the northern city of Adria.

Adrianna

(alt. Adriana)

Variant of Adrienne, meaning 'rich' or 'dark'.

Adrienne

(alt. Adriane, Adrianne)

Greek, meaning 'rich', or Latin meaning 'dark'.

Aegle

Greek, meaning 'brightness' or 'splendour'.

Aerin

Variant of Erin, meaning 'peace-making'.

Aerith

American, with no definitive meaning.

Aero
(alt. Aeron)

Meaning 'water'.

Aerolynn

Combination of the Greek Aero, meaning 'water', and the English Lynn, meaning 'waterfall'.

Africa

Celtic for 'pleasant', as well as the name of the continent.

Afsaneh

Iranian, meaning 'a fairy tale'.

Afsha

Persian, meaning 'one who sprinkles light'.

Afton

Originally a place name in Scotland.

Agatha

From Saint Agatha, the patron saint of bells, meaning 'good'.

Aglaia

One of the three Greek Graces, meaning 'brilliance'.

Agnes

Greek, meaning 'virginal' or 'pure'.

Agrippina

From the Latin expression, meaning 'born feet first'.

Aida

'Reward' or 'present' in Arabic.

Aidanne
(alt. Aidan, Aidenn)

Gaelic for 'fire'.

Ailbhe

Irish, meaning 'noble' or 'bright'.

Aileen
(alt. Aelinn, Aleen, Aline, Alline, Eileen)

A Gaelic variant of Helen, meaning 'light'.

Ailith
(alt. Ailish)

Old English, meaning 'seasoned warrior'.

Ailsa

Scottish, meaning 'pledge from God', as well as the name of a Scottish island.

Aimee
(alt. Aimie, Amie)

The French spelling of Amy, meaning 'beloved'.

Aina

Scandinavian, meaning 'forever'.

Aine
(alt. Aino)

Celtic for 'happiness'.

Ainsley

Scottish and Gaelic, meaning 'one's own meadow'.

Aisha
(alt. Aeysha)

In Arabic Aisha means 'woman'; in Swahili it means 'life'.

Aishwarya

Variant on the Arabic Aisha, meaning 'woman'.

Aislinn
(alt. Aislin, Aisling, Aislyn, Alene, Allene)

Irish Gaelic, meaning 'dream'.

Aiyanna
(alt. Aiyana)

Native American, meaning 'forever flowering'.

Aja

Hindi, meaning 'goat'.

Akela
(alt. Akilah)

Hawaiian, meaning 'noble'.

Akilina

Greek or Russian, meaning 'eagle'.

Akiva

Hebrew, meaning 'protect and shelter'.

Alaina

(alt. Alane, Alani, Alayna, Aleena)

Feminine of Alan, originating from the French for 'rock' or 'comely'.

Alana

(alt. Alanna, Alannah)

Variant of Alaina, meaning 'rock' or 'comely'.

Alanis

(alt. Alarice)

Variant of Alaina, meaning 'rock' or 'comely'.

Alba

Latin for 'white'.

Alberta

(alt. Albertha, Albertine)

Feminine of Albert, from the old English for 'bright and shining'.

Albina

Latin for 'white' or 'fair'.

Alda

German, meaning 'old' or 'prosperous'.

Aldis

English, meaning 'battle-seasoned'.

Aleta

(alt. Aletha)

Greek for 'footloose'.

Alethea

(alt. Aletheia)

Greek, meaning 'truth'.

Alex

(alt. Alexa, Alexi, Alexia, Alexina)

Shortened version of Alexandra, meaning 'man's defender'.

Alexandra

(alt. Alejandra, Alejandrina, Alejhandra, Aleksandra, Alessandra, Alexandrea, Alexandria, Aliandra)

Feminine of Alexander, from the Greek interpretation of 'man's defender'.

Alexis

(alt. Alexus, Alexys)

Greek, meaning 'helper'.

Aleydis

Variant of Alice, meaning 'nobility'.

Alfreda

Old English, meaning 'elf power'.

Ali

(alt. Allie, Ally)

Shortened version of Alexandra, Aliyah or Alice.

Alibeth

Variant of Elizabeth, meaning 'pledged to God'.

Alice

(alt. Alize, Alyce, Alys, Alyse)

English, meaning 'noble' or 'nobility'.

Alicia

(alt. Ahlicia, Alecia, Alesia, Alessia, Alizia, Alycia, Alysia)

Variant of Alice, meaning 'nobility'.

Alida

(alt. Aleida)

Latin, meaning 'small winged one'.

Alienor

(alt. Aliana)

Variant spelling of Eleanor, from the Greek for 'light'.

Aliki

(alt. Alika)

Variant of Alice, meaning 'nobility'.

Alima

Arabic, meaning 'cultured'.

Alina

(alt. Alena)

A Slavic variation of Helen, meaning 'light'.

Alisha

(alt. Alesha, Alysha)

Variant of Alice, meaning 'nobility'.

Alison

(alt. Allison, Allisyn, Allyson, Alyson)

Variant of Alice, meaning 'nobility'.

Alivia

Variant spelling of Olivia, meaning 'olive tree'.

Aliya
(alt. Aaliyah, Aleah, Alia, Aliah, Aliyah)

Arabic, meaning 'exalted' or 'sublime'.

Alla
Variant of Ella or Alexandra. Also a possible reference to Allah.

Allegra
Italian, meaning 'joyous'.

Allura
From the French word for entice, meaning 'the power of attraction'.

Allyn
Feminine of Alan, meaning 'peaceful'.

Alma
Three possible origins: Latin for 'giving nurture', Italian for 'soul' and Arabic for 'learned'.

Almeda
(alt. Almeta)

Latin, meaning 'ambitious'.

Almera
(alt. Almira)

Feminine of Elmer, from the Arabic for 'aristocratic'.

Alohi
Variant of the Hawaiian greeting Aloha, meaning 'love and affection'.

Alona
Hebrew, meaning 'oak tree'.

Alora
Variant of Alona, meaning 'oak tree'.

Alpha
The first letter of the Greek alphabet, usually given to a first-born daughter.

Alta
Latin, meaning 'elevated'.

Altagracia
Spanish, meaning 'grace'.

Althea
(alt. Altea, Altha)

From the Greek term, meaning 'healing power'.

A

Alva

Spanish, meaning 'blonde' or 'fair skinned'.

Alvena

(alt. Alvina)

English, meaning 'noble friend'.

Alvia

(alt. Alyvia)

Variant of Olivia or Elvira.

Alyssa

(alt. Alisa, Alissa, Allyssa, Alysa)

Greek, meaning 'rational'.

Amabel

Variant of Annabel, meaning 'grace and beauty'.

Amadea

Feminine of Amadeus, meaning 'God's beloved'.

Amalia

Variant of Emilia, meaning 'industrious'.

Amana

Hebrew, meaning 'loyal and true'.

Amanda

Latin, meaning 'much loved'.

Amandine

Variant of Amanda, meaning 'much loved'.

Amara

(alt. Amani)

Greek, meaning 'lovely forever'.

Amarantha

Contraction of Amanda and Samantha, meaning 'much loved listener'.

Amaris

(alt. Amari, Amasa, Amata, Amaya)

Hebrew, meaning 'pledged by God'.

Amaryllis

Greek, meaning 'fresh'. Also a flower by the same name.

Amber

From the French word for the semi-precious stone of the same name.

Amberly

Contraction of Amber and Leigh, meaning 'stone' and 'meadow'.

Amberlynn

Contraction of Amber and Lynn, meaning 'stone' and 'waterfall'.

Amelia

(alt. Aemilia)

Greek, meaning 'industrious'.

Amelie

(alt. Amalie)

French version of Amelia, meaning 'industrious'.

America

From the country of the same name.

Ameris

Variant of amaryllis, meaning 'fresh'.

Amethyst

From the Greek word for the precious, mulberry coloured stone of the same name.

Amina

Arabic, meaning 'honest and trustworthy'.

Amira

(alt. Amiya, Amiyah)

Arabic, meaning 'a highborn girl'.

Amity

Latin, meaning 'friendship and harmony'.

Amory

Variant on the Spanish name Amor, meaning 'love'.

Amy

(alt. Amee, Ami, Amie, Ammie)

Latin, meaning 'beloved'.

Amya

Variant of Amy, meaning 'beloved'.

Ana-Lisa

Contraction of Anna and Lisa, meaning 'gracious' or 'consecrated to God'.

Anafa

Hebrew, meaning 'heron'.

Ananda

Hindi, meaning 'bliss'.

Anastasia
(alt. Athanasia)

Greek, meaning 'resurrection'.

Anatolia

From the eastern Greek town of the same name.

Andelyn

Contraction of the feminine for Andrew and Lynn, meaning 'strong waterfall'.

Andrea
(alt. Andreia, Andria)

Feminine of Andrew, from the Greek term for 'a man's woman'.

Andrine

Variant of Andrea, meaning 'a man's woman'.

Andromeda

From the heroine of a Greek legend.

Anemone

Greek, meaning 'breath'.

Angela
(alt. Angel, Angeles, Angelia Angelle, Angie)

Greek, meaning 'messenger from God' or 'angel'.

Angelica
(alt. Angelina, Angeline, Angelique, Angelise, Angelita, Anjelica)

Latin, meaning 'angelic'.

Anise
(alt. Anisa, Anissa)

From the licorice flavoured plant of the same name.

Anita
(alt. Anitra)

Variant of Ann, meaning 'grace'.

Ann
(alt. Anne, Annie)

Derived from Hannah, meaning 'grace'.

Anna
(alt. Ana)

Derived from Hannah, meaning 'grace'.

Annabel

(alt. Anabel, Anabelle, Annabell,
Annabella, Annabelle)

Contraction of Anna and Belle,
meaning 'grace' and 'beauty'.

Annalise

(alt. Annalee, Annaliese,
Annalisa, Anneli, Annelie,
Annelies, Annelise)

Contraction of Anna and Lise,
meaning 'grace' and 'pledged
to God'.

Annemarie

(alt. Annamae, Annamarie,
Annelle, Annmarie)

Contraction of Anna and Mary,
meaning 'grace' and 'bitterness
or rebellious'.

Annette

(alt. Annetta)

Derived from Anna and
Hannah, meaning 'grace'.

Annis

Greek, meaning 'finished or
completed'.

Annora

Latin, meaning 'honour'.

Anoushka

(alt. Anousha)

A Russian variation of Ann,
meaning 'grace'.

Ansley

English, meaning 'the awesome
one's meadow'.

Anthea

(alt. Anthi)

Greek, meaning 'flowerlike'.

Antigone

In Greek mythology, Antigone
was the daughter of Oedipus.

Antoinette

(alt. Anonetta, Antonette,
Antonietta)

Both a variation of Ann and the
feminine of Anthony, meaning
'invaluable grace'.

Antonia

(alt. Antonella, Antonina)

Latin, meaning 'invaluable'.

Anwen

Welsh, meaning 'very fair'.

Anya
(alt. Aniya, Aniyah, Aniylah, Anja)
Russian, meaning 'grace'.

Apollonia
Feminine of Apollo, the Greek god of the sun.

Apple
Name of the fruit.

April
(alt. Avril)
Latin, meaning 'opening up'. Also the name of the month.

Aquilina
(alt. Aqua, Aquila)
Spanish, meaning 'like an eagle'.

Ara
Arabic, meaning 'brings rain'.

Arabella
Latin, meaning 'answered prayer'.

Araceli
(alt. Aracely)
Spanish, meaning 'altar of Heaven'.

Araminta
Contraction of Arabella and Amita, meaning 'altar of Heaven' and 'friendship'.

Arcadia
Greek, meaning 'paradise'.

Ardelle
(alt. Ardell, Ardella)
Latin, meaning 'burning with enthusiasm'.

Arden
(alt. Ardis, Ardith)
Latin, meaning 'burning with enthusiasm'.

Arella
(alt. Areli, Arely)
Hebrew, meaning 'angel'.

Aretha
Greek, meaning 'woman of virtue'.

A

Aria
(alt. Ariah)
Italian, meaning 'melody'.

Ariadne
In Greek mythology, Ariadne was the daughter of King Minos.

Ariana
(alt. Ariane, Arianna, Arienne)
Welsh, meaning 'silver'.

Ariel
(alt. Ariela, Ariella, Arielle)
Hebrew, meaning 'lioness of God'.

Arlene
(alt. Arleen, Arlie, Arline, Arly)
Gaelic, meaning 'pledge'.

Armida
Latin, meaning 'little armed one'.

Artemisia
(alt. Artemis)
Of both Greek and Spanish origin, meaning 'perfect'.

Artie
(alt. Arti)
Shortened form of Artemisia, meaning 'perfect'.

Ashanti
Geographical area in Africa

Ashby
English, meaning 'ash tree farm'. Also name of place in Leicestershire.

Ashley
(alt. Ashely, Ashlee, Ashleigh, Ashli, Ashlie, Ashly)
English, meaning 'ssh tree meadow'.

Ashlynn
(alt. Ashlyn)
Irish Gaelic, meaning 'dream'.

Ashton
(alt. Ashtyn)
Place name.

Asia
Name of continent.

A

Asma
(alt. Asmara)

Arabic, meaning 'high-standing'.

Aspen
(alt. Aspynn)

Name of the tree. Also name of a city in the USA.

Assumpta
(alt. Assunta)

Italian, meaning 'raised up'.

Asta
(alt. Asteria, Astor, Astoria)

Greek or Latin, meaning 'star-like'.

Astrid

Old Norse, meaning 'beautiful like a God'.

Atara

Hebrew, meaning 'diadem'.

Athena
(alt. Athenais)

The Greek goddess of wisdom.

Aubrey
(alt. Aubree, Aubriana, Aubrie)

French, meaning 'elf ruler'.

Audrey
(alt. Audra, Audrie, Audrina, Audry, Autry)

English, meaning 'noble strength'.

Augusta
(alt. August, Augustine)

Latin, meaning 'worthy of respect'.

Aura
(alt. Aurea)

Greek or Latin, meaning either 'soft breeze' or 'gold'.

Aurelia
(alt. Aurelie)

Latin, meaning gold.

Aurora
(alt. Aurore)

In Roman mythology, Aurora was the goddess of sunrise.

Austine
(alt. Austen, Austin)
Latin, meaning 'worthy of respect'.

Autumn
Name of the season

Ava
(alt. Avia, Avie)
Latin, meaning 'like a bird'.

Avalon
(alt. Avalyn, Aveline)
Celtic, meaning 'island of apples'.

Axelle
Greek, meaning 'father of peace.'

Aya
(alt. Ayah)
Hebrew, meaning 'bird'.

Ayanna
(alt. Ayana)
American, meaning 'grace'.

Ayesha
(alt. Aisha, Aysha)
Persian, meaning 'small one'.

Azalea
Latin, meaning 'dry earth'.

Azalia
Hebrew, meaning 'aided by God'.

Aziza
Hebrew, meaning 'mighty', or Arabic meaning 'precious'.

Azure
(alt. Azaria)
French, meaning 'sky-blue'.

Popular French names for boys and girls
Adele
Alain
Alphonse
Belle
Fleur
Jacques
Marc
Matthieu
Paulette
Sabine

A

B Girls' names

Babette

French version of Barbara, from the Greek word meaning 'foreign'.

Bailey
(alt. Baeli, Bailee)

English, meaning 'law enforcer'.

Bambi

Shortened version of the Italian Bambina, meaning 'child'.

Barbara
(alt. Barb, Barbie, Barbra)

Greek, meaning 'foreign'.

Basma

Arabic, meaning 'smile'.

Bathsheba

Hebrew, meaning 'daughter of the oath'.

Bay
(alt. Baya)

Plant or geographical name.

Beata

Latin, meaning 'blessed'.

Beatrice
(alt. Beatrix, Beatriz, Bellatrix, Betrys)

Latin, meaning 'bringer of gladness'.

Becky
(alt. Beccie, Beccy, Beckie)

Shortened form of Rebecca, meaning 'noose'.

Literary names

Alice (*Alice in Wonderland*, Lewis Carroll)
Beth (*Little Women*, Louisa M Alcott)
Cora (*Last of the Mohicans*, James Fenimore Cooper)
Darryl (*Malory Towers* series, Enid Blyton)
Eliza (*Pygmalion*, George Bernard Shaw)
Gwendolen (*The Importance of Being Earnest*, Oscar Wilde)
Hermione (*Harry Potter* series, J K Rowling)
Matilda (*Matilda*, Roald Dahl)
Miranda (*The Tempest*, William Shakespeare)
Wendy (*Peter Pan*, J M Barrie)

Bee
Shortened form of Beatrice, meaning 'bringer of gladness'.

Belinda
(*alt. Belen, Belina*)
Contraction of Belle and Linda, meaning 'beautiful'.

Bell
Shortened form of Isabel, meaning 'pledged to God'.

Bella
Latin, meaning 'beautiful'.

Belle
French, meaning 'beautiful'.

Belva
Latin, meaning 'beautiful view'.

Bénédicta
Latin, the feminine of Benedict, meaning 'blessed'.

Benita
(*alt. Bernita*)
Spanish, meaning 'blessed'.

Bennie
Shortened version of Bénédicta and Benita.

B

218

Berit
(alt. Beret)

Scandinavian, meaning 'splendid' or 'gorgeous'.

Bernadette

French, meaning 'courageous'.

Bernadine

French, meaning 'courageous'.

Bernice
(alt. Berenice, Berniece, Burnice)

Greek, meaning 'she who brings victory'.

Bertha
(alt. Berta, Berthe, Bertie)

German origin, meaning 'bright'.

Beryl

Greek, meaning 'pale, green gemstone'.

Bess
(alt. Bessie)

Shortened form of Elizabeth, meaning 'consecrated to God'.

Beth

Hebrew, meaning 'house'. Also shortened form of Elizabeth, meaning 'consecrated to God'.

Bethany
(alt. Bethan)

Biblical, referring to a geographical location.

Bethel

Hebrew, meaning 'house of God'.

Bettina

Spanish version of Elizabeth, meaning 'consecrated to God'.

Betty
(alt. Betsy, Bette, Bettie, Bettye)

Shortened version of Elizabeth, meaning 'consecrated to God'.

Beulah

Hebrew, meaning 'married'.

Beverly
(alt. Beverlee, Beverley)

English, meaning 'beaver stream'.

B

Beyoncé

American, made popular by the singer.

Bianca
(alt. Blanca)

Italian, meaning 'white'.

Bijou

French, meaning 'precious ring'.

Billie
(alt. Bill, Billy, Billye)

Shortened version of Wilhelmina, meaning 'determined'.

Bina

Hebrew, meaning 'knowledge'.

Birgit
(alt. Birgitta)

Norwegian, meaning 'splendid'.

Blair

Scottish Gaelic, meaning 'flat, plain area'.

Blake
(alt. Blakely, Blakelyn)

English, meaning either 'pale-skinned' or 'dark'.

Blanche
(alt. Blanch)

French, meaning 'white or pale'.

Bliss

English, meaning 'intense happiness'.

Blithe

English, meaning 'joyous'.

Blodwen

Welsh, meaning 'white flower'.

Blossom

English, meaning 'flowerlike'.

Blythe
(alt. Bly)

English, meaning 'happy and carefree'.

Bobbi
(alt. Bobbie, Bobby)

Shortened version of Roberta, meaning 'famous brilliance'.

B

Bonita

Spanish, meaning 'pretty'.

Bonnie

(alt. Bonny)

Scottish, meaning 'fair of face'.

Brandy

(alt. Brandee, Brandi, Brandie)

Name of the liquor.

Brea

(alt. Bree, Bria)

Shortened form of Brianna, meaning 'strong'.

Brenda

English, meaning 'burning or stinking hair'.

Brianna

(alt. Breana, Breann, Breanna, Breanne, Brenna, Brenyn, Briana, Brianne, Bryanna)

Irish Gaelic, meaning 'strong'.

Bridget

(alt. Bridgett, Bridgette, Brigette, Brigid, Brigitta, Brigitte)

Irish Gaelic, meaning 'strength and power'.

Brier

French, meaning 'heather'.

Brit

(alt. Britt, Britta)

Celtic, meaning 'spotted' or 'freckled'.

Britannia

Latin, meaning 'Britain'.

Brittany

(alt. Britany, Britney, Britni, Brittani, Brittanie, Brittney, Brittni, Brittny)

Latin, meaning 'from England'.

Biblical names

Elizabeth
Eve
Hannah
Leah
Mary
Miriam
Rachel
Rebecca
Ruth
Sarah

B

Bronwyn
(alt. Bronwen)

Welsh, meaning 'fair breast'.

Brooke
(alt. Brook)

English, meaning 'small stream'.

Brooklyn
(alt. Brooklynn)

Name of a New York borough.

Brunhilda

German, meaning 'armour-wearing fighting maid'.

Bryn
(alt. Brynn)

Welsh, meaning 'mount'.

Bryony
(alt. Briony)

Name of a European vine.

Popular Indian names for boys and girls

Ajay
Bharat
Deepal
Haresh
Jaya
Manisha
Paresh
Rabiya
Ravi
Sunita

B

C Girls' names

Cadence
Latin, meaning 'with rhythm'.

Cai
Vietnamese, meaning 'feminine'.

Caitlin
(alt. Cadyn, Caitlann, Caitlyn, Caitlynn)
Greek, meaning 'pure'.

Calandra
Greek, meaning 'lark'.

Calantha
(alt. Calanthe)
Greek, meaning 'lovely flower'.

Caledonia
Latin, meaning 'from Scotland'.

Calla
Greek, meaning 'beautiful'.

Callie
(alt. Caleigh, Cali, Calleigh, Cally)
Greek, meaning 'beauty'.

Calliope
From the muse of epic poetry in Greek mythology.

Callista
(alt. Callisto)
Greek, meaning 'most beautiful'.

Camas

Native American, from the root and bulb of the same name.

Cambria

Welsh, from the alternative name of the same country.

Camden

(alt. Camdyn)

English, meaning 'winding valley'.

Cameo

Italian, meaning 'skin'.

Cameron

(alt. Camryn)

Scottish Gaelic, meaning 'bent nose'.

Camilla

(alt. Camelia, Camellia, Camila, Camillia)

Latin, meaning 'spiritual serving girl'.

Camille

Latin, meaning 'spiritual serving girl'.

Candace

(alt. Candice, Candis)

Latin, meaning 'brilliant white'.

Candida

Of Latin origin, meaning 'white'.

Candra

Latin, meaning 'glowing'.

Candy

(alt. Candi)

Shortened form of Candace, meaning 'brilliant white'.

Caoimhe

Celtic, meaning 'gentleness'.

Caprice

Italian, meaning 'ruled by whim'.

Cara

Latin, meaning 'darling'.

Caren

(alt. Carin, Caron, Caryn)

Greek, meaning 'pure'.

C

Carey
(alt. Cari, Carie, Carri, Carrie, Cary)
Welsh, meaning 'near the castle'.

Carina
(alt. Corina)
Italian, meaning 'dearest little one'.

Carissa
(alt. Carisa)
Greek, meaning 'grace'.

Carla
(alt. Charla)
Feminine of the German Carl, meaning 'man'.

Carlin
(alt. Carleen, Carlene)
Gaelic, meaning 'little champion'.

Carlotta
(alt. Carlota)
Italian, meaning 'free man'.

Carly
(alt. Carlee, Carley, Carli, Carlie)
Feminine of the German Charles, meaning 'man'.

Carmel
(alt. Carmela, Carmelita, Carmella)
Hebrew, meaning 'garden'.

Carmen
(alt. Carma, Carmina)
Latin, meaning 'song'.

Carol
(alt. Carole, Carrol, Carroll, Caryl)
Shortened form of Caroline, meaning 'man'.

Caroline
(alt. Carolann, Carolina, Carolyn, Carolynn)
German, meaning 'man'.

Carrington
English, meaning 'Charles's town'.

C

Saints' names

Ada
Agatha
Catherine
Felicity
Helena
Joan
Lydia
Margaret
Mary
Teresa

Carys
(alt. Cerys)
Welsh, meaning 'love'.

Casey
Irish Gaelic, meaning 'watchful'.

Cassandra
(alt. Casandra, Cassandre)
Greek, meaning 'one who prophesies doom'.

Cassia
(alt. Casia, Casie, Cassie)
Greek, meaning 'cinnamon'.

Cassidy
Irish, meaning 'clever'.

Catalina
(alt. Catarina, Caterina)
Spanish version of Catherine, meaning 'pure'.

Catherine
(alt. Catharine, Cathrine, Cathryn)
Greek, meaning 'pure'.

Cathleen
Irish version of Catherine, meaning 'pure'.

Cathy
(alt. Cathey, Cathi, Cathie)
Shortened form of Catherine, meaning 'pure'.

Caty
(alt. Caddie, Caitee, Cate, Catie)
Shortened form of Catherine, meaning 'pure'.

Cayley
(alt. Cayla, Caylee, Caylen)
American, meaning 'pure'.

C

Cecilia
(alt. Cecelia, Cecily, Cicely, Cicily)

Latin, meaning 'blind one'.

Cecile
(alt. Cecilie)

Latin, meaning 'blind one'.

Celena

Greek, meaning 'goddess of the moon'.

Celeste
(alt. Celestina, Celestine)

Latin, meaning 'heavenly'.

Celine
(alt. Celia, Celina)

French version of Celeste, meaning 'heavenly'.

Cerise

French, meaning 'cherry'.

Chanah

Hebrew, meaning 'grace'.

Chandler
(alt. Chandell)

English, meaning 'candle maker'.

Chandra
(alt. Chanda, Chandry)

Sanskrit, meaning 'like the moon'.

Chanel
(alt. Chanelle)

French, from the designer of the same name.

Chantal
(alt. Chantel, Chantelle, Chantilly)

French, meaning 'stony spot'.

Chardonnay

French, from the wine variety of the same name.

Charis
(alt. Charissa, Charisse)

Greek, meaning 'grace'.

Charity

Latin, meaning 'brotherly love'.

Charlene
(alt. Charleen, Charline)

German, meaning 'man'.

C

Charlie
(alt. Charlee, Charley Charlize, Charly)
Shortened form of Charlotte, meaning 'little and feminine'.

Charlotte
(alt. Charnette, Charolette)
French, meaning 'little and feminine'.

Charmaine
Latin, meaning 'clan'.

Chastity
Latin, meaning 'purity'.

Chava
(alt. Chaya)
Hebrew, meaning 'beloved'.

Chelsea
(alt. Chelsee, Chelsey, Chelsi, Chelsie)
English, meaning 'port or landing place'.

Cher
French, meaning 'beloved'.

Cherie
(alt. Cheri, Cherise)
French, meaning 'dear'.

Cherish
(alt. Cherith)
English, meaning 'to treasure'.

TV personality names

Alexa (Chung)
Amanda (Holden)
Cheryl (Cole)
Davina (McCall)
Fern/e (Britton, Cotton)
Holly (Willoughby)
Kirstie (Allsopp)
Myleene (Klass)
Tess (Daly)

C

Chermona

Hebrew, meaning 'sacred mountain'.

Cherry

(alt. Cherri)

French, meaning 'cherry fruit'.

Cheryl

(alt. Cheryle)

English, meaning 'little and womanly'.

Chesney

English, meaning 'place to camp'.

Cheyenne

(alt. Cheyanne)

Native American, from the tribe of the same name.

Chiara

(alt. Ceara, Chiarina, Ciara)

Italian, meaning 'light'.

China

From the country of the same name.

Chiquita

Spanish, meaning 'little one'.

Chloe

(alt. Cloe)

Greek, meaning 'pale green shoot'.

Chloris

Of Greek origin, meaning 'pale'.

Chris

(alt. Chrissy, Christa, Christie, Christy, Crissy, Cristy)

Shortened form of Christina, meaning 'anointed Christian'.

Christabel

Both Latin and French, meaning 'fair Christian'.

Christina

(alt. Christiana, Cristina)

Greek, meaning 'anointed Christian'.

Christine

(alt. Christeen, Christen, Christene, Christian, Christiane, Christin)

Greek, meaning 'anointed Christian'.

Chuma

Aramaic, meaning 'warmth'.

C

Cierra
(alt. Ciera)

Irish, meaning 'black'.

Cinderella

French, meaning 'little ash-girl'.

Cindy
(alt. Cinda, Cindi, Cyndi)

Shortened form of Cynthia, meaning 'goddess'.

Cinnamon

Greek, from the spice of the same name.

Citlali
(alt. Citlalli)

Aztec, meaning 'star'.

Citrine

Latin, from the gemstone of the same name.

Claire
(alt. Clare)

Latin, meaning 'bright'.

Clara
(alt. Claira)

Latin, meaning 'bright'.

Clarabelle
(alt. Claribel)

Contraction of Clara and Isobel, meaning 'bright' and 'consecrated to God'.

Clarissa
(alt. Clarice, Clarisse)

Variation of Claire, meaning 'bright'.

Clarity

Latin, meaning 'lucid'.

Claudette

Latin, meaning 'lame'.

Claudia
(alt. Claudie, Claudine)

Latin, meaning 'lame'.

Clematis

Greek, meaning 'vine'.

Clementine
(alt. Clemency, Clementina, Clemmie)

Latin, meaning 'mild and merciful'.

Cleopatra

Greek, meaning 'her father's renown'.

Clio

(alt. Cleo, Cliona)

Greek, from the muse of history of the same name.

Clodagh

Irish, meaning 'river'.

Clotilda

(alt. Clothilda, Clothilde, Clotilde)

German, meaning 'renowned battle'.

Clover

English, from the flower of the same name.

Coco

Spanish, meaning 'help'.

Cody

English, meaning 'pillow'.

Colleen

(alt. Coleen)

Irish Gaelic, meaning 'girl'.

Collette

(alt. Colette)

Greek and French, meaning 'people of victory'.

Connie

Latin, meaning 'steadfast'.

Constance

(alt. Constanza)

Latin, meaning 'steadfast'.

Consuelo

(alt. Consuela)

Spanish, meaning 'comfort'.

Cora

Greek, meaning 'maiden'.

Coral

(alt. Coralie, Coraline, Corelia, Corene)

Latin, from the marine life of the same name.

Corazon

Spanish, meaning 'heart'.

Cordelia

(alt. Cordia, Cordie)

Latin, meaning 'heart'.

Corey

(alt. Cori, Corrie, Cory)

Irish Gaelic, meaning 'the hollow'.

C

Corin
(alt. Corine)
Latin, meaning 'spear'.

Corinne
(alt. Corinna, Corrine)
French version of Cora, meaning 'maiden'.

Corliss
English, meaning 'cheery'.

Cornelia
Latin, meaning 'like a horn'.

Cosette
French, meaning 'people of victory'.

Cosima
(alt. Cosmina)
Greek, meaning 'order'.

Courtney
(alt. Cortney)
English, meaning 'court-dweller'.

Creola
French, meaning 'American-born, English descent'.

Crescent
French, meaning 'increasing'.

Cressida
From the heroine in Greek mythology of the same name.

Crystal
(alt. Christal, Chrystal, Cristal)
Greek, meaning 'ice'.

Csilla
Hungarian, meaning 'defences'.

Cynara
Greek, meaning 'thistly plant'.

Cynthia
Greek, meaning 'goddess from the mountain'.

Cyra
Persian, meaning 'sun'.

Cyrilla
Latin, meaning 'lordly'.

C

D Girls' names

Dacey
Irish Gaelic, meaning 'from the south'.

Dada
Nigerian, meaning 'curly haired'.

Dagmar
German, meaning 'day's glory'.

Dagny
Nordic, meaning 'new day'.

Dahlia
Scandinavian, from the flower of the same name.

Dai
Japanese, meaning 'great'.

Daisy
(alt. Dasia)
English, meaning 'eye of the day'.

Dakota
Native American, meaning 'allies'.

Dalia
(alt. Dalila)
Hebrew, meaning 'delicate branch'.

Dallas
Scottish Gaelic, from the village of the same name. Also city in America.

Damaris

Greek, meaning 'calf'.

Damita

Spanish, meaning 'little noblewoman'.

Dana

(alt. Dania, Danna, Dayna)

English, meaning 'from Denmark'.

Danae

Greek, from the mythological heroine of the same name.

Danica

(alt. Danika)

Latin, meaning 'from Denmark'.

Danielle

(alt. Danelle, Daniela, Daniella, Danila, Danyelle)

The feminine form of the Hebrew Daniel, meaning 'God is my judge'.

Danita

English, meaning 'God will judge'.

Daphne

(alt. Dafne, Daphna)

Of Greek origin, meaning 'laurel tree'.

Dara

Hebrew and Persian, meaning 'wisdom'.

Darby

(alt. Darbi, Darbie)

Irish, meaning 'park with deer'.

Darcie

(alt. Darci, Darcy)

Irish Gaelic, meaning 'dark'.

Daria

Greek, meaning 'rich'.

Darla

English, meaning 'darling'.

Darlene

(alt. Darleen, Darline)

American, meaning 'darling'.

Daryl

(alt. Darryl)

English, originally used as a surname.

D

Davina
Hebrew, meaning 'loved one'.

Dawn
(alt. Dawna)
English, meaning 'the dawn'.

Daya
Hebrew, meaning 'bird of prey'.

Deanna
(alt. Dayana, Deana, Deanna, Deanne)
English, meaning 'valley'.

Debbie
(alt. Debbi, Debby, Debi)
Shortened form of Deborah, meaning 'bee'.

Deborah
(alt. Debbra, Debora, Debra, Debrah)
Hebrew, meaning 'bee'.

December
Latin, meaning 'tenth month'.

Dee
Welsh, meaning 'swarthy'.

Deidre
(alt. Deidra, Deirdre)
Irish, meaning 'raging woman'.

Deja
(alt. Dejah)
French, meaning 'already'.

Delaney
Irish Gaelic, meaning 'offspring of the challenger'.

Delia
Greek, meaning 'from Delos'.

Delilah
(alt. Delina)
Hebrew, meaning 'seductive'.

Della
(alt. Dell)
Shortened form of Adele, meaning 'nobility'.

Delores
(alt. Deloris)
Spanish, meaning 'sorrows'.

Delphine
(alt. Delpha, Delphia, Delphina, Delphinia)
Greek, meaning 'dolphin'.

D

Delta

Greek, meaning 'fourth child'.

Demetria

(alt. Demetrice)

Greek, from the mythological heroine of the same name.

Demi

French, meaning 'half'.

Dena

(alt. Deena)

English, meaning 'from the valley'.

Denise

(alt. Denice, Denisa, Denisse)

French, meaning 'follower of Dionysius'.

Desdemona

Greek, meaning 'wretchedness'.

Desiree

(alt. Desirae)

French, meaning 'much desired'.

Desma

Greek, meaning 'blinding oath'.

Destiny

(alt. Destany, Destinee, Destiney, Destini)

French, meaning 'fate'.

Deva

Hindi, meaning 'God-like'.

Devin

(alt. Devinne)

Irish Gaelic, meaning 'poet'.

Devon

English, from the county of the same name.

Diamond

English, meaning 'brilliant'.

Diana

(alt. Dian, Diane, Dianna, Dianne)

Roman, meaning 'divine'.

Diandra

Greek, meaning 'two males'.

Dilys

Welsh, meaning 'reliable'.

Uncommon three syllable names

Annabel
Cassandra
Evelyn
Gloria
Harriet
India
Priscilla
Tamara
Vanessa

Dimitra

Greek, meaning 'follower of Demeter'.

Dimona

Hebew, meaning 'south'.

Dinah

(alt. Dina)

Hebrew, meaning 'justified'.

Dionne

Greek, from the mythological heroine of the same name.

Divine

Italian, meaning 'heavenly'.

Dixie

French, meaning 'tenth'.

Dodie

Hebew, meaning 'well-loved'.

Dolly

(alt. Dollie)

Shortened form of Dorothy, meaning 'gift of 'God'.

Dolores

(alt. Doloris)

Spanish, meaning 'sorrows'.

Dominique

(alt. Domenica, Dominica, Domonique)

Latin, meaning 'Lord'.

D

237

Donata

Latin, meaning 'given'.

Donna

(alt. Dona, Donnie)

Italian, meaning 'lady'.

Dora

Greek, meaning 'gift'.

Dorcas

Greek, meaning 'gazelle'.

Doreen

(alt. Dorene, Dorine)

Irish Gaelic, meaning 'brooding'.

Doris

(alt. Dorris)

Greek, from the place of the same name.

Dorothy

(alt. Dorathy, Doretha, Dorotha, Dorothea, Dorthy)

Greek, meaning 'gift of God'.

Dorrit

(alt. Dorit)

Greek, meaning 'gift of God'.

Dory

(alt. Dori)

French, meaning 'gilded'.

Dottie

(alt. Dotty)

Shortened form of Dorothy, meaning 'gift of God'.

Dove

(alt. Dovie)

English, from the bird of the same name.

Drew

Greek, meaning 'masculine'.

Drusilla

(alt. Drucilla)

Latin, meaning 'of the Drusus clan'.

Dulcie

(alt. Dulce, Dulcia)

Latin, meaning 'sweet'.

Dusty

(alt. Dusti)

English, from the place of the same name.

E Girls' names

Earla
English, meaning 'leader'.

Eartha
English, meaning 'earth'.

Easter
Egyptian, from the festival of the same name.

Ebba
English, meaning 'fortress of riches'.

Ebony
(alt. Eboni)

Latin, meaning 'deep, black wood'.

Echo
Greek, from the mythological nymph of the same name.

Eda
(alt. Edda)

English, meaning 'wealthy and happy'.

Edelmira
Spanish, meaning 'admired for nobility'.

Eden
Hebrew, meaning 'pleasure'.

Edie
(alt. Eddie)

Shortened form of Eden, meaning 'pleasure'.

Edina

Scottish, meaning 'from Edinburgh'.

Edith
(alt. Edyth)

English, meaning 'prosperity through battle'.

Edna

Hebrew, meaning 'enjoyment'.

Edrea

English, meaning 'wealthy and powerful'.

Edwina

English, meaning 'wealthy friend'.

Effie

Greek, meaning 'pleasant speech'.

Eglantine

French, from the shrub of the same name.

Eibhlín

Irish Gaelic, meaning 'shining and brilliant'.

Eileen

Irish, meaning 'shining and brilliant'.

Ekaterina
(alt. Ekaterini)

Slavic, meaning 'pure'.

Elaine
(alt. Elaina, Elayne)

French, meaning 'bright, shining light'.

Elba

Italian, from the island of the same name.

Elberta

English, meaning 'highborn'.

Eldora

Spanish, meaning 'covered with gold'.

Eleanor
(alt. Elana, Elanor, Eleanora, Eleanore, Elena, Eleni, Elenor, Elenora, Eliana, Elina, Elinor, Elinore)

Greek, meaning 'light'.

Electra
(alt. Elektra)

Greek, meaning 'shining', also from the myth.

Elfrida
(alt. Elfrieda)

English, meaning 'elf power'.

Eliane

Hebrew, meaning 'Jehovah is God'.

Elissa
(alt. Elisa)

Of French origin, meaning 'pledged to God'.

Eliza
(alt. Elisha)

Of Hebrew origin, meaning 'pledged to God'.

Elizabeth
(alt. Elisabet, Elisabeth, Elizabella, Elizabelle, Elsbeth, Elspeth)

Hebrew, meaning 'pledged to God'.

Elke

German, meaning 'nobility'.

Ella

German, meaning 'completely'.

Elle
(alt. Ellie)

French, meaning 'she'.

Ellen
(alt. Elin, Eline, Ellyn)

Greek, meaning 'shining'.

Ellice
(alt. Elyse)

Greek, meaning 'the Lord is God'.

Elma
(alt. Elna)

Latin, meaning 'soul'.

Elmira

Arabic, meaning 'aristocratic lady'.

Elodie

French, meaning 'marsh flower'.

Eloise
(alt. Elois, Eloisa, Elouise)

French, meaning 'renowned in battle'.

E

Elsa
(alt. Else, Elsie)

Hebrew, meaning 'pledged to God'.

Elva
Irish, meaning 'noble'.

Elvina
English, meaning 'noble friend'.

Elvira
(alt. Elvera)

Spanish, from the place of the same name.

Ember
(alt. Embry)

English, meaning 'spark'.

Emeline
German, meaning 'industrious'.

Emerald
English, meaning 'green gemstone'.

Emery
German, meaning 'ruler of work'.

Emilia
Latin, meaning 'from the Emily clan'.

Emily
(alt. Emalee, Emelie, Emely, Emilee, Emilie, Emlyn)

Latin, from the clan of the same name.

Emma
German, meaning 'embraces everything'.

Emmanuelle
Hebrew, meaning 'God is among us'.

Emmeline
(alt. Emmelina)

German, meaning 'embraces everything'.

Emmy
(alt. Emi, Emme, Emmie)

German, meaning 'embraces everything'.

Ena
Shortened form of Georgina, meaning 'farmer'.

E

Enid
(alt. Eneida)
Welsh, meaning 'life spirit'.

Enola
Native American, meaning 'solitary'.

Enya
Irish Gaelic, meaning 'fire'.

Erica
(alt. Ericka, Erika)
Scandinavian, meaning 'ruler forever'.

Erin
(alt. Eryn)
Irish Gaelic, meaning 'from the isle to the west'.

Eris
Greek, from the mythological heroine of the same name.

Erlinda
Hebrew, meaning 'spirited'.

Erma
German, meaning 'universal'.

Ermine
French, meaning 'weasel'.

Erna
English, meaning 'sincere'.

Ernestine
(alt. Ernestina)
English, meaning 'sincere'.

Esme
French, meaning 'esteemed'.

Esmeralda
Spanish, meaning 'emerald'.

Esperanza
Spanish, meaning 'hope'.

Estelle
(alt. Estela, Estell, Estella)
French, meaning 'star'.

Esther
(alt. Esta, Ester, Etha, Ethna, Ethne)
Persian, meaning 'star'.

Eternity
Latin, meaning 'forever'.

E

Ethel
(alt. Ethyl)
English, meaning 'noble'.

Etta
(alt. Etter, Ettie)
Shortened form of Henrietta, meaning 'ruler of the house'.

Eudora
Greek, meaning 'generous gift'.

Eugenia
(alt. Eugenie)
Greek, meaning 'wellborn'.

Eulalia
(alt. Eula, Eulah, Eulalie)
Greek, meaning 'sweet-speaking'.

Eunice
Greek, meaning 'victorious'.

Euphemia
Greek, meaning ' favourable speech'.

Eva
Hebrew, meaning 'life'.

Evadne
Greek, meaning 'pleasing one'.

Evangeline
(alt. Evangelina)
Greek, meaning 'good news'.

Evanthe
Greek, meaning 'good flower'.

Eve
(alt. Evie)
Hebrew, meaning 'life'.

Evelina
(alt. Evelia)
German, meaning 'hazelnut'.

Evelyn
(alt. Evalyn, Evelin, Eveline, Evelyne)
German, meaning 'hazelnut'.

Everly
(alt. Everleigh, Everley)
English, meaning 'grazing meadow'.

Evette
French, meaning 'yew wood'.

Evonne
(alt. Evon)
French, meaning 'yew wood'.

E

F

Girls' names

Fabia
(alt. Fabiana, Fabienne, Fabiola, Fabriana)

Latin, meaning 'from the Fabian clan'.

Fabrizia
Italian, meaning 'works with hands'.

Faith
English, meaning 'loyalty'.

Faiza
Of Arabic origin, meaning 'victorious'.

Fallon
Irish Gaelic, meaning 'descended from a ruler'.

Fanny
(alt Fannie)

Latin, meaning 'from France'.

Farica
German, meaning 'peaceful ruler'.

Farrah
English, meaning 'lovely and pleasant'.

Fatima
Arabic, from the daughter of Mohammed with the same name.

Faustine
Latin, meaning 'fortunate'.

Fawn

French, meaning 'young deer'.

Fay

(alt. Fae, Faye)

French, meaning 'fairy'.

Felicia

(alt. Felecia, Felice, Felicita, Felisha)

Latin, meaning 'lucky and happy'.

Felicity

Latin, meaning 'fortunate'.

Old name, new fashion?

Bella
Carolyn
Clara
Dorothy
Emmeline
Hazel
Matilda
Nora
Penelope
Rosalie

Fenella

Irish Gaelic, meaning 'white shoulder'.

Fenia

Scandinavian, from the mythological giantess of the same name.

Fern

(alt. Ferne, Ferrin)

English, from the plant of the same name.

Fernanda

German, meaning 'peace and courage'.

Ffion

(alt. Fion)

Irish Gaelic, meaning 'fair and pale'.

Fia

Italian, meaning 'flame'.

Fifi

Hebrew, meaning 'Jehovah increases'.

Filomena

Greek, meaning 'loved one'.

F

Finlay
(alt. Finley)

Irish Gaelic, meaning 'fair-headed courageous one'.

Finola
(alt. Fionnula)

Irish Gaelic, meaning 'fair shoulder'.

Fiona

Irish Gaelic, meaning 'fair and pale'.

Fiora

Irish Gaelic, meaning 'fair and pale'.

Flanna
(alt. Flannery)

Irish Gaelic, meaning 'russet hair'.

Flavia

Latin, meaning 'yellow hair'.

Fleur

French, meaning 'flower'.

Flo
(alt. Florrie, Flossie, Floy)

Shortened forms of Florence, meaning 'in bloom'.

Flora

Latin, meaning 'flower'.

Florence
(alt. Florencia, Florene, Florine)

Latin, meaning 'in bloom'.

Florida

Latin, meaning 'flowery'. Also a state in America.

Fran
(alt.Frankie, Frannie)

Shortened form of Frances, meaning 'from France'.

Frances
(alt. Francine, Francis)

Latin, meaning 'from France'.

Francesca
(alt. Franchesca, Francisca)

Latin, meaning 'from France'.

F

Freda

(alt. Freeda, Freida, Frida, Frieda)

German, meaning 'peaceful'.

Frederica

German, meaning 'peaceful ruler'.

Fuchsia

German, from the flower of the same name.

Names of poets

Adrienne (Rich)
Anne (Sexton)
Carol Ann (Duffy)
Charlotte (Perkins Gilman)
Emily (Dickinson)
Erica (Jong)
Maya (Angelou)
Pam (Ayres)
Sylvia (Plath)
Wendy (Cope)

F

G Girls' names

Gabby
(alt. Gabbi)
Shortened form of Gabrielle, meaning 'heroine of God'.

Gabrielle
(alt. Gabriel, Gabriela, Gabriella)
Hebrew, meaning 'heroine of God'.

Gaia
(alt. Gaea)
Greek, meaning 'the earth'.

Gail
(alt. Gale, Gayla, Gayle)
Hebrew, meaning 'my father rejoices'.

Gala
French, meaning 'festive merrymaking'.

Galiena
German, meaning 'high one'.

Galina
Russian, meaning 'shining brightly'.

Garnet
(alt. Garnett)
English, meaning 'red gemstone'.

Gay
(alt. Gaye)
French, meaning 'glad and lighthearted'.

Gaynor

Welsh, meaning 'white and smooth'.

Gemini

Greek, meaning 'twin'.

Gemma

Italian, meaning 'precious stone'.

Gene

Greek, meaning 'wellborn'.

Genesis

Greek, meaning 'beginning'.

Geneva
(alt. Genevra)

French, meaning 'juniper tree'.

Genevieve

German, meaning 'white wave'.

Genie

Shortened form of Genevieve, meaning 'white wave'.

Georgette

French, meaning 'farmer'.

Names from ancient Rome

Aggripina
Antonia
Claudia
Drusilla
Honorata
Hortensia
Narcissa
Romana
Tatiana
Valeria

Georgia
(alt. Georgiana, Georgianna, Georgie)

Latin, meaning 'farmer'.

Georgina
(alt. Georgene, Georgine, Giorgina)

Latin, meaning 'farmer'.

Geraldine

German, meaning 'spear ruler'.

Gerda

Nordic, meaning 'shelter'.

Geri
(alt. Gerri, Gerry)

Shortened form of Geraldine, meaning 'spear ruler'.

Germaine

French, meaning 'from Germany'.

Gertie

Shortened form of Gertrude, meaning 'strength of a spear'.

Gertrude

German, meaning 'strength of a spear'.

Gia
(alt. Ghia)

Italian, meaning 'God is gracious'.

Gianina
(alt. Giana)

Hebrew, meaning 'God's graciousness'.

Gigi
(alt. Giget)

Shortened form of Georgina, meaning 'farmer'.

Gilda

English, meaning 'gilded'.

Gilia

Hebrew, meaning 'joy of the Lord'.

Gillian

Latin, meaning 'youthful'.

Gina
(alt. Geena, Gena)

Shortened form of Regina, meaning 'queen'.

Ginger

Latin, from the root of the same name.

Ginny

Shortened form of Virginia, meaning 'virgin'.

Giovanna

Italian, meaning 'God is gracious'.

Giselle
(alt. Gisela, Gisele, Giselle, Gisselle)

German, meaning 'pledge'.

G

Gita
(alt. Geeta)
Sanskrit, meaning 'song'.

Giulia
(alt. Giuliana)
Italian, meaning 'youthful'.

Gladys
(alt. Gladyce)
Welsh, meaning 'lame'.

Glenda
Welsh, meaning 'fair and good'.

Glenna
(alt. Glennie)
Irish Gaelic, meaning 'glen'.

Gloria
(alt. Glory)
Latin, meaning 'glory'.

Glynda
(alt. Glinda)
Welsh, meaning 'fair'.

Glynis
Welsh, meaning 'small glen'.

Golda
(alt. Goldia, Goldie)
English, meaning 'gold'.

Grace
(alt. Graça, Gracie, Gracin, Grayce)
Latin, meaning 'grace'.

Grainne
(alt. Grania)
Irish Gaelic, meaning 'love'.

Gratia
(alt. Grasia)
Latin, meaning 'blessing'.

Greer
(alt. Grier)
Latin, meaning 'alert and watchful'.

Gregoria
Latin, meaning 'alert'.

Greta
(alt. Gretel)
Greek, meaning 'pearl'.

Gretchen
German, meaning 'pearl'.

G

Griselda
(alt. Griselle)

German, meaning 'grey fighting maid'.

Gudrun

Scandinavian, meaning 'battle'.

Guinevere

Welsh, meaning 'white and smooth'.

Gwen

Shortened form of Gwendolyn, meaning 'fair bow'.

Gwenda

Welsh, meaning 'fair and good'.

Gwendolyn
(alt. Gwendolen, Gwenel)

Welsh, meaning 'fair bow'.

Gwynn
(alt. Gwyn)

Welsh, meaning 'fair blessed'.

Gwyneth
(alt. Gwynneth, Gwynyth)

Welsh, meaning 'happiness'.

Gypsy

English, meaning 'of the Roman tribe'.

Names from ancient Greece

Alexandra
Apollonia
Corinna
Irene
Lysandra
Melaina
Pelagia
Sophia
Xenia
Zenobia

G

Popular Irish names for boys and girls

Aidan
Aisling
Connor
Declan
Deidre
Eileen
Kieran
Liam
Niamh
Siobhan

H Girls' names

Hadassah
Hebrew, meaning 'myrtle tree'.

Hadley
English, meaning 'heather meadow'.

Hadria
Latin, meaning 'from Adria'.

Hala
Arabic, meaning 'halo'.

Haley
(alt. Haelee, Haely, Hailee, Hailey, Hailie, Haleigh, Hali, Halie)
English, meaning 'hay meadow'.

Halima
(alt. Halina)
Arabic, meaning 'gentle'.

Hallie
(alt. Halle, Halley, Hallie)
German, meaning 'ruler of the home or estate'.

Hannah
(alt. Haana, Hana, Hanna)
Hebrew, meaning 'grace'.

Harley
(alt. Harlene)
English, meaning 'the long field'.

Harlow
English, meaning 'army hill'.

255

Harmony

Latin, meaning 'harmony'.

Harper

English, meaning 'minstrel'.

Harriet
(alt. Harriett, Harriette)

German, meaning 'ruler of the home or estate'.

Hattie

Shortened form of Harriet, meaning 'ruler of the home or estate'.

Haven

English, meaning 'a place of sanctuary'.

Hayden

English, meaning 'hedged valley'.

Hayley
(alt. Haylee, Hayleigh, Haylie)

English, meaning 'hay meadow'.

Hazel
(alt. Hazle)

English, from the tree of the same name.

Heather

English, from the flower of the same name.

Heaven

English, meaning 'everlasting bliss'.

Hedda

German, meaning 'warfare'.

Hedwig

German, meaning 'warfare and strife'.

Heidi
(alt. Heidy)

German, meaning 'nobility'.

Helen
(alt. Halen, Helena, Helene, Hellen)

Greek, meaning 'light'.

Helga

German, meaning 'holy and sacred'.

Names with positive meanings

Belle – Beautiful
Blythe – Carefree
Felicity – Happy
Lakshmi – Good
Lucy – Light
Millicent – Brave
Mira – Wonderful
Rinah – Joyful
Sunny – Sunshine
Yoko – Positive

Heloise

French, meaning 'renowned in war'.

Henrietta

(alt. Henriette)

German, meaning 'ruler of the house'.

Hephzibah

Hebrew, meaning 'my delight is in her'.

Hera

Greek, meaning 'queen'.

Hermia

(alt. Hermina, Hermine, Herminia)

Greek, meaning 'messenger'.

Hermione

Greek, meaning 'earthly'.

Hero

Greek, meaning 'brave one of the people'.

Hertha

English, meaning 'earth'.

Hesper

Greek, meaning 'evening star'.

Hester
(alt. Hestia)
Greek, meaning 'star'.

Hilary
(alt. Hillary)
Greek, meaning 'cheerful and happy'.

Hilda
(alt. Hildur)
German, meaning 'battle woman'.

Hildegarde
(alt. Hildegard)
German, meaning 'battle stronghold'.

Hildred
German, meaning 'battle counsellor'.

Hilma
German, meaning 'will-helmet'.

Hollis
English, meaning 'near the holly bushes'.

Holly
(alt. Holli, Hollie)
English, from the tree of the same name.

Honey
English, meaning 'honey'.

Honor
(alt. Honour)
Latin, meaning 'woman of honour'.

Honora
(alt. Honoria)
Latin, meaning 'woman of honour'.

Hope
English, meaning 'hope'.

Hortense
(alt. Hortencia, Hortensia)
Latin, meaning 'of the garden'.

Hulda
German, meaning 'loved one'.

Hyacinth
Greek, from the flower of the same name.

Girls' names

Iantha
Greek, meaning 'purple flower'.

Ida
English, meaning 'prosperous'.

Idell
(alt. Idella)
English, meaning 'prosperous'.

Idona
Nordic, meaning 'renewal'.

Ignacia
Latin, meaning 'ardent'.

Ila
French, meaning 'island'.

Ilana
Hebrew, meaning 'tree'.

Ilaria
Italian, meaning 'cheerful'.

Ilene
American, meaning 'light'.

Iliana
(alt. Ileana)
Greek, meaning 'Trojan'.

Ilona
Hungarian, meaning 'light'.

Ilsa
German, meaning 'pledged to God'.

Ima

German, meaning 'embraces everything'.

Iman

Arabic, meaning 'faith'.

Imelda

German, meaning 'all-consuming fight'.

Imogen
(alt. Imogene)

Latin, meaning 'last-born'.

Ina

Latin, meaning 'to make feminine'.

Inaya

Arabic, meaning 'taking care'.

India
(alt. Indie)

Hindi, from the country of the same name.

Indiana

Latin, meaning 'from India'.

Indigo

Greek, meaning 'deep blue dye'.

Indira
(alt. Inira)

Sanskrit, meaning 'beauty'.

Inez
(alt. Ines)

Spanish, meaning 'pure'.

Inga
(alt. Inge, Ingeborg, Inger)

Scandinavian, meaning 'guarded by Ing'.

Ingrid

Scandinavian, meaning 'beautiful'.

Io

Greek, from the mythological heroine of the same name.

Ioanna

Greek, meaning 'grace'.

Iola
(alt. Iole)

Greek, meaning 'cloud of dawn'.

Iolanthe

Greek, meaning 'violet flower'.

Iona

Greek, from the island of the same name.

Ione

Greek, meaning 'violet'.

Iphigenia

Greek, meaning 'sacrifice'.

Ira
(alt. Iva)

Hebrew, meaning 'watchful'.

Irene
(alt. Irelyn, Irena, Irina, Irini)

Greek, meaning 'peace'.

Iris

Greek, meaning 'rainbow'.

Irma

German, meaning 'universal'.

Isabel
(alt. Isabela, Isabell, Isabella, Isabelle, Isabeth, Isobel, Izabella, Izabelle)

Spanish, meaning 'pledged to God'.

Isadora

Latin, meaning 'gift of Isis'.

Ishana

Hindi, meaning 'desire'.

Isis

Egyptian, from the goddess of the same name.

Isla
(alt. Isa, Isela, Isley)

Scottish Gaelic, meaning 'river'.

Isolde

Welsh, meaning 'fair lady'.

Ivana

Slavic, meaning 'Jehovah is gracious'.

Ivette

Variation of Yvette, meaning 'yew wood'.

Ivonne

Variation of Yvonne, meaning 'yew wood'.

Ivory

Latin, meaning 'white as elephant tusks'.

Ivy

English, from the plant of the same name.

Ixia

South African, from the flower of the same name.

Boys' names for girls (female spellings)

Ashley
Billie
Casey
Charlie
Elliott
Geri
Jamie
Jordan
Leigh
Toni

J Girls' names

Jacinda
(alt. Jacinta)
Spanish, meaning 'hyacinth'.

Jackie
(alt. Jacque, Jacqui)
Shortened form of Jacqueline, meaning 'he who supplants'.

Jacqueline
(alt. Jacalyn, Jacklyn, Jaclyn, Jacquelin, Jacquelyn, Jacquline, Jaqlyn, Jaquelin, Jaqueline)
French, meaning 'he who supplants'.

Jade
(alt. Jada, Jaida, Jayda, Jayde)
Spanish, meaning 'green stone'.

Jaden
(alt. Jadyn, Jaiden, Jaidyn, Jayden)
Contraction of Jade and Hayden, meaning 'green hedged valley'.

Jael
Hebrew, meaning 'mountain goat'.

Jaime
(alt. Jaima, Jaimie, Jami, Jamie)
Spanish, meaning 'he who supplants'.

Jamila
Arabic, meaning 'lovely'.

Jan
(alt. Jann, Janna)

Hebrew, meaning 'the Lord is gracious'.

Jana
(alt. Jaana)

Hebrew, meaning 'the Lord is gracious'.

Janae
(alt. Janay)

American, meaning 'the Lord is gracious'.

Jane
(alt. Jayne)

Feminine form of the Hebrew John, meaning 'the Lord is gracious'.

Janelle
(alt. Janel, Janell, Jenelle)

American, meaning 'the Lord is gracious'.

Janet
(alt. Janette)

Scottish, meaning 'the Lord is gracious'.

Janice
(alt. Janis)

American, meaning 'the Lord is gracious'.

Janie
(alt. Janney, Jannie)

Shortened form of Janet, meaning 'the Lord is gracious'.

Janine
(alt. Janeen)

English, meaning 'the Lord is gracious'.

Janoah
(alt. Janiya, Janiyah)

Hebrew, meaning 'quiet and calm'.

January

English, meaning 'the first month'.

Jasmine
(alt. Jasmin, Jazim, Jazmine)

Persian, meaning 'jasmine flower'.

Jay

Latin, meaning 'jaybird'.

J

Jayna

Sanskrit, meaning 'bringer of victory'.

Jean

(alt. Jeane, Jeanne)

Scottish, meaning 'the Lord is gracious'.

Jeana

(alt. Jeanna)

Latin, meaning 'queen'.

Jeanette

(alt. Jeannette, Janette)

French, meaning 'the Lord is gracious'.

Flower names

Daisy
Flora
Heather
Hyacinth
Iris
Lily
Poppy
Primrose
Rose
Violet

Jeanie

(alt. Jeannie)

Shortened form of Jeanette, meaning 'the Lord is gracious'.

Jeanine

(alt. Jeannine)

Latin, meaning 'the Lord is gracious'.

Jemima

Hebrew, meaning 'dove'.

Jemma

Italian, meaning 'precious stone'.

Jena

Arabic, meaning 'little bird'.

Jenna

Hebrew, meaning 'the Lord is gracious'.

Jennifer

(alt. Jenifer)

Welsh, meaning 'white and smooth'.

J

Jenny
(alt. Jennie)

Shortened form of Jennifer, meaning 'white and smooth'.

Jerrie
(alt. Jeri, Jerri, Jerrie, Jerry)

German, meaning 'spear ruler'.

Jerusha

Hebrew, meaning 'married'.

Jeryl

English, meaning 'spear ruler'.

Jessa

Shortened form of Jessica, meaning 'He sees'.

Jessamy
(alt. Jessame, Jessamine, Jessamyn)

Persian, meaning 'jasmine flower'.

Jessica
(alt. Jesica, Jesika, Jessika)

Hebrew, meaning 'He sees'.

Jessie
(alt. Jesse, Jessi, Jessye)

Shortened form of Jessica, meaning 'He sees'.

Jesusa

Spanish, meaning 'mother of the Lord'.

Jette
(alt. Jetta, Jettie)

Danish, meaning 'black as coal'.

Jewel
(alt. Jewell)

French, meaning 'delight'.

Jezebel
(alt. Jezabel, Jezabelle)

Hebrew, meaning 'pure and virginal'.

Jill

Latin, meaning 'youthful'.

Jillian

Latin, meaning 'youthful'.

Jimena

Spanish, meaning 'heard'.

J

Jo

Shortened form of Joanna, meaning 'the Lord is gracious'.

Joan

Hebrew, meaning 'the Lord is gracious'.

Joanna

(alt. Joana, Joanie, Joann, Joanne, Johanna, Joni)

Hebrew, meaning 'the Lord is gracious'.

Jocasta

Italian, meaning 'lighthearted'.

Jocelyn

(alt. Jauslyn, Jocelyne, Joscelin, Joslyn)

German, meaning 'cheerful'.

Jody

(alt. Jodee, Jodi, Jodie)

Shortened form of Judith, meaning 'Jewish'.

Joelle

(alt. Joela)

Hebrew, meaning 'Jehovah is the Lord'.

Joie

French, meaning 'joy'.

Jolene

Contraction of Joanna and Darlene, meaning 'gracious darling'.

Jolie

(alt. Joely)

French, meaning 'pretty'.

Jordan

(alt. Jordana, Jordin, Jordyn)

Hebew, meaning 'descend'.

Josephine

(alt. Josefina, Josephina)

Hebrew, meaning 'Jehovah increases'.

Josie

(alt. Joss, Jossie)

Shortened form of Josephine, meaning 'Jehovah increases'.

Jovita

(alt. Jovie)

Latin, meaning 'made glad'.

Joy

Latin, meaning 'joy'.

J

Joyce
Latin, meaning 'joyous'.

Juanita
(alt. Juana)
Spanish, meaning 'the Lord is gracious'.

Judith
(alt. Judit)
Hebrew, meaning 'Jewish'.

Judy
(alt. Judi, Judie)
Shortened form of Judith, meaning 'Jewish'.

Jules
French, meaning 'Jove's child'.

Julia
Latin, meaning 'youthful'.

Julianne
(alt. Juliana, Juliann, Julianne)
Latin, meaning 'youthful'

Julie
(alt. Juli)
Shortened form of Julia, meaning 'youthful'.

Juliet
(alt. Joliet, Juliette)
Latin, meaning 'youthful'.

June
(alt. Juna)
Latin, after the month of the same name.

Juniper
Dutch, from the shrub of the same name.

Juno
(alt. Juneau)
Latin, meaning 'queen of heaven'.

Justice
English, meaning 'to deliver what is just'.

Justine
(alt. Justina)
Latin, meaning 'fair and righteous'.

Jørgina
Dutch, meaning 'farmer'.

K Girls' names

Kadenza
(alt. Kadence)
Latin, meaning 'with rhythm'.

Kaitlin
(alt. Kaitlyn)
Greek, meaning 'pure'.

Kala
(alt. Kaela, Kaiala, Kaila)
Sanskrit, meaning 'black one'.

Kali
*(alt. Kailee, Kailey, Kaleigh,
Kaley, Kalie, Kalli, Kally, Kaylee,
Kayleigh)*
Sanskrit, meaning 'black one'.

Kalila
Arabic, meaning 'beloved'.

Kalina
Slavic, meaning 'flower'.

Kalliope
Greek, from the muse of the
same name.

Kallista
Greek, meaning 'most
beautiful'.

Kama
Sanskrit, meaning 'love'.

Kami
Japanese, meaning 'lord'.

Kamilla
(alt. Kamilah)
Slavic, meaning 'serving girl'.

Place names

Ailsa
Alexandria
Brittany
Eden
India
Lydia
Martinique
Normandie
Paris
Skye

Kana

Hawaiian, from the demi-god of the same name.

Kandace
(alt. Kandice)

Latin, meaning 'glowing white'.

Kandy
(alt. Kandi)

Shortened form of Kandace, meaning 'glowing white'.

Kara

Latin, meaning 'dear one'.

Karen
(alt. Karan, Karalyn, Karin, Karina, Karon, Karren)

Greek, meaning 'pure'.

Kari
(alt. Karie, Karri, Karrie)

Shortened form of Karen, meaning 'pure'.

Karimah

Arabic, meaning 'giving'.

Karishma

Sanskrit, meaning 'miracle'.

Karla

German, meaning 'man'.

Karly
(alt. Karlee, Karley, Karli)

German, meaning 'free man'.

Karlyn

German, meaning 'man'.

Karma

Hindi, meaning 'destiny'.

Karol
(alt. Karolina, Karolyn)
Slavic, meaning 'little and womanly'.

Kasey
(alt. Kacey, Kaci, Kacie, Kacy, Kasie, Kassie)
Irish Gaelic, meaning 'alert and watchful'.

Kassandra
Greek, meaning 'she who entangles men'.

Katarina
(alt. Katarine, Katerina, Katharina)
Greek, meaning 'pure'.

Kate
(alt. Kat, Katie, Kathi, Kathie, Kathy, Kati, Katy)
Shortened form of Katherine, meaning 'pure'.

Katelyn
(alt. Katelin, Katelynn, Katlin, Katlyn)
Greek, meaning 'pure'.

Katherine
(alt. Katharine, Katheryn, Kathrine, Kathryn)
Greek, meaning 'pure'.

Kathleen
(alt. Kathlyn)
Greek, meaning 'pure'.

Katrina
(alt. Katina)
Greek, meaning 'pure'.

Kay
(alt. Kaye)
Shortened form of Katherine, meaning 'pure'.

Kayla
(alt. Kaylah)
Greek, meaning 'pure'.

Kayley
(alt. Kayley, Kayli)
American, meaning 'pure'.

Kaylin
American, meaning 'pure'.

Keeley
(alt. Keely)
Irish, meaning 'battle maid'.

271

Keila
Hebrew, meaning 'citadel'.

Keira
Irish Gaelic, meaning 'dark'.

Keisha
(alt. Keesha)
Arabic, meaning 'woman'.

Kelis
American, meaning 'beautiful'.

Kelly
(alt. Keli, Kelley, Kelli, Kellie)
Irish Gaelic, meaning 'battle maid'.

Kelsey
(alt. Kelcee, Kelcie, Kelsea, Kelsi, Kelsie)
English, meaning 'island'.

Kendall
(alt. Kendal)
English, meaning 'the valley of the Kent'.

Kendra
English, meaning 'knowing'.

Kenna
Irish Gaelic, meaning 'handsome'.

Kennedy
(alt. Kenadee, Kennedi)
Irish Gaelic, meaning 'helmet head'.

Kenya
African, from the country of the same name.

Kerensa
Cornish, meaning 'love'.

Kerrigan
Irish, meaning 'black haired'.

Kerry
(alt. Keri, Kerri, Kerrie)
Irish, from the county of the same name.

Khadijah
(alt. Khadejah)
Arabic, meaning 'premature baby'.

Kiana
(alt. Kia, Kiana)
American, meaning 'fibre'.

Kiara

Italian, meaning 'light'.

Kiki

Spanish, meaning 'home ruler'.

Kim

Shortened form of Kimberly, from the town of the same name.

Kimberly
(alt. Kimberleigh, Kimberley)

English, from the South African town of the same name.

Kingsley
(alt. Kinsley)

English, meaning 'king's meadow'.

Kinsey

English, meaning 'king's victory'.

Kira

Greek, meaning 'lady'.

Kiri

Maori, meaning 'tree bark'.

> ## Long names
>
> Alexandria
> Bernadette
> Christabelle
> Constantine
> Evangeline
> Gabrielle
> Henrietta
> Jacqueline
> Marguerite
> Wilhelmina

Kirsten
(alt. Kirstin)

Scandinavian, meaning 'Christian'.

Kirstie
(alt. Kirsty)

Shortened form of Kirsten, meaning 'Christian'.

Kitty
(alt. Kittie)

Shortened form of Katherine, meaning 'pure'.

Kizzy

Hebrew, meaning 'Cassia'.

Klara

Hungarian, meaning 'bright'.

Komal

Hindi, meaning 'soft and tender'.

Konstantina

Latin, meaning 'steadfast'.

Kora
(alt. Kori)

Greek, meaning 'maiden'.

Kris
(alt. Krista, Kristi, Kristie, Kristy)

Shortened form of Kristen, meaning 'Christian'.

Kristen
(alt. Kristan, Kristin, Kristine, Krysten)

Greek, meaning 'Christian'.

Krystal
(alt. Kristal, Kristel)

Greek, meaning 'ice'.

Kwanza
(alt. Kwanzaa)

African, meaning 'beginning'.

Kyla
(alt. Kya, Kylah, Kyle)

Scottish, meaning 'narrow spit of land'.

Kylie
(alt. Kiley, Kylee)

Irish Gaelic, meaning 'graceful'.

Kyra

Greek, meaning 'lady'.

Kyrie

Greek, meaning 'the Lord'.

Short names

Bea
Bo
Fay
Jan
Jo
Kay
Kim
May
Mia
Val

L Girls' names

Lacey
(alt. Laci, Lacie, Lacy)
French, from the town of the same name.

Ladonna
Italian, meaning 'lady'.

Lady
English, meaning 'bread kneader'.

Laila
(alt. Laelia, Layla, Leila, Lela, Lelah, Lelia)
Arabic, meaning 'night'.

Lainey
(alt. Laine, Laney)
French, meaning 'bright light'.

Lakeisha
(alt. Lakeshia)
American, meaning 'woman'.

Lakshmi
(alt. Laxmi)
Sanskrit, meaning 'good omen'.

Lana
Greek, meaning 'light'.

Lani
(alt. Lanie)
Hawaiian, meaning 'sky'.

Lara
Latin, meaning 'famous'.

Laraine

French, meaning 'from Lorraine'.

Larissa
(alt. Larisa)
Greek, meaning 'lighthearted'.

Lark
(alt. Larkin)
English, meaning 'playful songbird'.

Larsen

Scandinavian, meaning 'son of Lars'.

Latifa

Arabic, meaning 'gentle and pleasant'.

Latika

Hindi, meaning 'a plant'.

Latisha

Latin, meaning 'happiness'.

Latona
(alt. Latonia)
Roman, from the mythological heroine of the same name.

Latoya

Spanish, meaning 'victorious one'.

Latrice
(alt. Latricia)
Latin, meaning 'noble'.

Laura

Latin, meaning 'laurel'.

Laurel

Latin, meaning 'laurel tree'.

Lauren
(alt. Lauran, Loren)
Latin, meaning 'laurel'.

Laveda
(alt. Lavada)
Latin, meaning 'cleansed'.

Lavender

Latin, from the plant of the same name.

Laverne
(alt. Lavern, Laverna)
Latin, from the goddess of the same name.

Lavinia
(alt. Lavina)

Latin, meaning 'woman of Rome'.

Lavonne
(alt. Lavon)

French, meaning 'yew wood'.

Leah
(alt. Lea, Leia)

Hebrew, meaning 'weary'.

Leandra

Greek, meaning 'lion man'.

Leanne
(alt. Leann, Leanna, Leeann)

Contraction of Lee and Ann, meaning 'meadow grace'.

Leda

Greek, meaning 'gladness'.

Lee
(alt. Leigh)

English, meaning 'pasture or meadow'.

Leilani

Hawaiian, meaning 'flower from heaven'.

'Bad girl' names

Delilah
Desdemona
Jezebel
Lilith
Pandora
Roxy
Salome
Scarlett
Tallulah
Trixie

Leith

Scottish Gaelic, meaning 'broad river'.

Lena
(alt. Leena, Lina)

Latin, meaning 'light'.

Lenna
(alt. Lennie)

German, meaning 'lion's strength'.

Lenore
(alt. Lenora)

Greek, meaning 'light'.

277

Léonie
(alt. Leona, Leone)
Latin, meaning 'lion'.

Leonora
(alt. Leonor, Leonore)
Greek, meaning 'light'.

Leora
Greek, meaning 'light'.

Leslie
(alt. Leslee, Lesley, Lesli)
Scottish Gaelic, meaning 'the grey castle'.

Leta
Latin, meaning 'glad and joyful'.

Letha
Greek, meaning 'forgetfulness'.

Letitia
(alt. Leticia, Lettice, Lettie)
Latin, meaning 'joy and gladness'.

Lexia
(alt. Lexi)
Greek, meaning 'defender of mankind'.

Lia
Italian, meaning 'bringer of the gospel'.

Liana
French, meaning 'to twine around'.

Libby
(alt. Libbie)
Shortened form of Elizabeth, meaning 'pledged to God'.

Liberty
English, meaning 'freedom'.

Lida
Slavic, meaning 'loved by the people'.

Liese
(alt. Liesel, Liesl)
German, meaning 'pledged to God'.

Lila
(alt. Lilah)
Arabic, meaning 'night'.

Lilac
Latin, from the flower of the same name.

Lilia
(alt. Lilias)
Scottish, meaning 'lily'.

Lilith
Arabic, meaning 'ghost'.

Lillian
(alt. Lilian, Liliana, Lilla, Lillianna)
Latin, meaning 'lily'.

Lily
(alt. Lillie, Lilly)
Latin, from the flower of the same name.

Linda
(alt. Lynda)
Spanish, meaning 'pretty'.

Linden
(alt. Lindie, Lindy)
European, from the tree of the same name.

Lindsay
(alt. Lindsey, Linsey)
English, meaning 'island of linden trees'.

Linette
Welsh, meaning 'idol'.

Linnea
(alt. Linnae, Linny)
Scandinavian, meaning 'lime or linden tree'.

Liora
(alt. Lior)
Hebrew, meaning 'I have a light'.

Lisa
(alt. Leesa, Lise, Liza)
Hebrew, meaning 'pledged to God'.

Lissa
Greek, meaning 'bee'.

Lissandra
(alt. Lisandra)
Greek, meaning 'man's defender'.

Liv
Nordic, meaning 'defence'.

Livia
Latin, meaning 'olive'.

L

Famous female singers

Amy (Winehouse)
Billie (Holiday)
Elaine (Paige)
Ella (Fitzgerald)
Etta (James)
Judy (Garland)
Julie (Andrews)
Leona (Lewis)
Lily (Allen)
Nina (Simone)

Liz
(alt. Lizzie, Lizzy)
Shortened form of Elizabeth, meaning 'pledged to God'.

Logan
Irish Gaelic, meaning 'small hollow'.

Lois
Of German origin, meaning 'renowned in battle'.

Lola
Spanish, meaning 'sorrows'.

Lolita
Spanish, meaning 'sorrows'.

Lona
Latin, meaning 'lion'.

Lora
Latin, meaning 'laurel'.

Lorelei
(alt. Loralai, Loralie)
German, meaning 'dangerous rock'.

Lorenza
Latin, meaning 'from Laurentium'.

Loretta
(alt. Loreto)
Latin, meaning 'laurel'.

Lori
(alt. Laurie, Lorie, Lorri)
Latin, meaning 'laurel'.

Lorna
Scottish, from the place of the same name.

Lorraine

(alt. Loraine)

French, meaning 'from Lorraine'.

Lottie

(alt. Lotta, Lotte)

French, meaning 'little and womanly'.

Lotus

Greek, meaning 'lotus flower'.

Lou

(alt. Louie, Lue)

Shortened form of Louise, meaning 'renowned in battle'.

Louise

(alt. Louisa, Luisa)

German, meaning 'renowned in battle'.

Lourdes

French, from the town of the same name.

Love

English, meaning 'love'.

Lowri

Welsh, meaning 'crowned with laurels'.

Luanne

(alt. Luann, Luanna)

German, meaning 'renowned in battle'.

Lucia

(alt. Luciana)

Italian, meaning 'light'.

Lucille

(alt. Lucile, Lucilla)

French, meaning 'light'.

Lucinda

English, meaning 'light'.

Lucretia

(alt. Lucrece)

Spanish, meaning 'light'.

Lucy

(alt. Lucie)

Latin, meaning 'light'.

Ludmilla

Slavic, meaning 'beloved of the people'.

L

Luella

English, meaning 'renowned in battle'.

Lulu

(alt. Lula)

German, meaning 'renowned in battle'.

Luna

Latin, meaning 'moon'.

Lupe

Spanish, from the town of the same name.

Luz

Spanish, meaning 'light'.

Lydia

(alt. Lidia)

Greek, meaning 'from Lydia'.

Lynn

(alt. Lyn, Lynne)

Spanish, meaning 'pretty'.

Lyra

Latin, meaning 'lyre'.

Tennis players

Anna (Kournikova)
Billie Jean (King)
Chris (Evert)
Margaret (Smith Court)
Maria (Sharapova)
Martina (Hingis/
　Navrátilová)
Monica (Seles)
Serena (Williams)
Steffi (Graf)
Venus (Williams)

L

 Girls' names

Mab
Irish Gaelic, meaning 'joy'.

Mabel
(alt. Mabelle, Mable)
Latin, meaning 'loveable'.

Macaria
Spanish, meaning 'blessed'.

Macy
(alt. Macey, Maci, Macie)
French, meaning 'Matthew's estate'.

Mada
English, meaning 'from Magdala'.

Madden
(alt. Maddyn)
Irish, meaning 'little dog'.

Maddie
(alt. Maddi, Maddie, Madie)
Shortened form of Madeline, meaning 'from Magdala'.

Madeline
(alt. Madaline, Madalyn, Madeleine, Madelyn, Madelynn, Madilyn)
Greek, meaning 'from Magdala'.

Madge
Greek, meaning 'pearl'.

Madhuri
Hindi, meaning 'sweet girl'.

Madison
(alt. Maddison, Madisen, Madisyn, Madyson)
English, meaning 'son of the mighty warrior'.

Madonna
Latin, meaning 'my lady'.

Maeve
Irish Gaelic, meaning 'intoxicating'.

Mafalda
Spanish, meaning 'battle-mighty'.

Magali
Greek, meaning 'pearl'.

Magdalene
(alt. Magdalen, Magdalena)
Greek, meaning 'from Magdala'.

Maggie
Shortened form of Margaret, meaning 'pearl'.

Magnolia
Latin, from the flower of the same name.

Mahala
(alt. Mahalia)
Hebrew, meaning 'tender affection'.

Maia
(alt. Maja)
Greek, meaning 'mother'.

Maida
English, meaning 'maiden'.

Maisie
(alt. Maisey, Maisy, Maizie, Masie, Mazie)
Greek, meaning 'pearl'.

Malka
Hebrew, meaning 'queen'.

Mallory
(alt. Malorie)
French, meaning 'unhappy'.

Malvina
Gaelic, meaning 'smooth brow'.

Mamie
(alt. Mammie)
Shortened form of Margaret, meaning 'pearl'.

Mandy
(alt. Mandie)
Shortened form of Amanda, meaning 'much loved'.

Manisha
Sanskrit, meaning 'desire'.

Mansi
Hopi, meaning 'plucked flower'.

Manuela
Spanish, meaning 'the Lord is among us'.

Mara
Hebrew, meaning 'bitter'.

Marcela
(alt. Marceline, Marcella, Marcelle)
Latin, meaning 'war-like'.

Marcia
Latin, meaning 'war-like'.

Marcy
(alt. Marci, Marcie)
Latin, meaning 'war-like'.

Margaret
(alt. Margarete, Margaretta, Margarette, Margret)
Greek, meaning 'pearl'.

Margery
(alt. Marge, Margie, Margit, Margy)
French, meaning 'pearl'.

Margo
(alt. Margot)
French, meaning 'pearl'.

Marguerite
(alt. Margarita)
French, meaning 'pearl'.

Maria
(alt. Mariah)
Latin, meaning 'bitter'.

Marian
(alt. Mariam, Mariana, Marion)
French, meaning 'bitter grace'.

Marianne
(alt. Mariana, Mariann, Maryann, Maryanne)
French, meaning 'bitter grace'.

M

Maribel

American, meaning 'bitterly beautiful'.

Marie

French, meaning 'bitter'.

Mariel

(alt. Mariela, Mariella)

Dutch, meaning 'bitter'.

Marietta

(alt. Marieta)

French, meaning 'bitter'.

Marigold

English, from the flower of the same name.

Marika

Dutch, meaning 'bitter'.

Marilyn

(alt. Marilee, Marilene, Marilynn)

English, meaning 'bitter'.

Marin

American, from the county of the same name.

Marina

(alt. Marine)

Latin, meaning 'from the sea'.

Mariposa

Spanish, meaning 'butterfly'.

Maris

Latin, meaning 'of the sea'.

Marisa

Latin, meaning 'of the sea'.

Marisol

Spanish, meaning 'bitter sun'.

Marissa

American, meaning 'of the sea'.

Marjolaine

French, meaning 'marjoram'.

Marjorie

(alt. Marjory)

French, meaning 'pearl'.

Marla

Shortened form of Marlene, meaning 'bitter'.

Marlene
(alt. Marlen, Marlena)
Hebrew, meaning 'bitter'.

Marley
(alt. Marlee)
American, meaning 'bitter'.

Marlo
(alt. Marlowe)
American, meaning 'bitter'.

Marseille
French, from the city of the same name.

Marsha
English, meaning 'war-like'.

Martha
(alt. Marta)
Aramaic, meaning 'lady'.

Martina
Latin, meaning 'war-like'.

Marvel
French, meaning 'something to marvel at'.

Mary
Hebrew, meaning 'bitter'.

Masada
Hebrew, meaning 'foundation'.

Matilda
(alt. Mathilda, Mathilde, Matide)
German, meaning 'battle-mighty'.

Mattea
Hebrew, meaning 'gift of God'.

Maude
(alt. Maud)
German, meaning 'battle-mighty'.

Maura
Irish, meaning 'bitter'.

Maureen
(alt. Maurine)
Irish, meaning 'bitter'.

Mavis
French, meaning 'thrush'.

M

Maxine
(alt. Maxie)
Latin, meaning 'greatest'.

May
(alt. Mae, Maya, Maye, Mayra)
Hebrew, meaning 'gift of God'.
Also the month.

Mckenna
(alt. Mackenna)
Irish Gaelic, meaning 'son of
the handsome one'.

Mckenzie
*(alt. Mackenzie, Mckenzy,
Mikenzi)*
Irish Gaelic, meaning 'son of
the wise ruler'.

Medea
(alt. Meda)
Greek, meaning 'ruling'.

Meg
Shortened form of Margaret,
meaning 'pearl'.

Megan
(alt. Meagan, Meghan)
Welsh, meaning 'pearl'.

Mehitabel
Hebrew, meaning 'benefited
by God'.

Mehri
Persian, meaning 'kind'.

Melanie
(alt. Melania, Melany, Melonie)
Greek, meaning 'dark-skinned'.

Melba
Australian, meaning 'from
Melbourne'.

Melia
(alt. Meliah)
German, meaning 'industrious'.

Melina
Greek, meaning 'honey'.

Melinda
Latin, meaning 'honey'.

Melisande
French, meaning 'bee'.

Melissa
(alt. Melisa, Mellissa)
Greek, meaning 'bee'.

Melody
(alt. Melodie)
Greek, meaning 'song'.

Melvina
Celtic, meaning 'chieftain'.

Menora
Hebrew, meaning 'candlestick'.

Mercedes
Spanish, meaning 'mercies'.

Mercy
English, meaning 'mercy'.

Meredith
(alt. Meridith)
Welsh, meaning 'great ruler'.

Merle
French, meaning 'blackbird'.

Merry
English, meaning 'lighthearted'.

Meryl
(alt. Merrill)
Irish Gaelic, meaning 'sea-bright'.

Meta
German, meaning 'pearl'.

Mia
Italian, meaning 'mine'.

Michaela
(alt. Makaela, Makaila, Makayla, Micaela, Mikaela, Mikaila, Mikala, Mikayla)
Hebrew, meaning 'who is like the Lord'.

Michelle
(alt. Machelle, Mechelle, Michaele, Michal, Michele)
French, meaning 'who is like the Lord'.

Mickey
(alt. Mickie)
Shortened form of Michelle, meaning 'who is like the Lord'.

Migdalia
Greek, meaning 'from Magdala'.

Mignon
French, meaning 'cute'.

Mika
(alt. Micah)
Hebrew, meaning 'who resembles God'.

Milada
Czech, meaning 'my love'.

Milagros
Spanish, meaning 'miracles'.

Milan
Italian, from the city of the same name.

Mildred
English, meaning 'gentle strength'.

Milena
Czech, meaning 'love and warmth'.

Miley
American, meaning 'smiley'.

Millicent
German, meaning 'highborn power'.

Millie
(alt. Milly)
Shortened form of Millicent, meaning 'highborn power'.

Mimi
Italian, meaning 'bitter'.

Popular song names

Billie Jean (*Billie Jean*, Michael Jackson)
Caroline (*Sweet Caroline*, Neil Diamond)
Delilah (*Delilah*, Tom Jones)
Eileen (*Come on Eileen*, Dexy's Midnight Runners)
Eleanor (*Eleanor Rigby*, The Beatles)
Georgia (*Georgia on My Mind*, Ray Charles)
Rio (*Rio*, Duran Duran)
Rosemary (*Love Grows (Where My Rosemary Goes)*, Edison Lighthouse)
Roxanne (*Roxanne*, The Police)
Sally (*Mustang Sally*, Wilson Pickett)

M

Mina
(alt. Mena)
German, meaning 'love'.

Mindy
(alt. Mindi)
Latin, meaning 'honey'.

Minerva
Roman, from the goddess of the same name.

Ming
Chinese, meaning 'bright'.

Minna
German, meaning 'will-helmet'.

Minnie
German, meaning 'will-helmet'.

Mira
Latin, meaning 'admirable'.

Mirabel
(alt. Mirabella, Mirabelle)
Latin, meaning 'wonderful'.

Miranda
(alt. Meranda)
Latin, meaning 'admirable'.

Mirella
(alt. Mireille, Mirela)
Latin, meaning 'admirable'.

Miriam
Hebrew, meaning 'bitter'.

Mirta
Spanish, meaning 'crown of thorns'.

Missy
Shortened form of Melissa, meaning 'bee'.

Misty
(alt. Misti)
English, meaning 'mist'.

Mitzi
German, meaning 'bitter'.

Miu
Japanese, meaning 'beautiful feather'.

Moira
(alt. Maira)
Irish, meaning 'bitter'.

M

Molly
(alt. Mollie)
American, meaning 'bitter'.

Mona
Irish Gaelic, meaning 'aristocratic'.

Monica
(alt. Monika, Monique)
Latin, meaning 'adviser'.

Montserrat
(alt. Monserrate)
Spanish, from the town of the same name.

Morag
Scottish, meaning 'star of the sea'.

Morgan
(alt. Morgann)
Welsh, meaning 'great and bright'.

Moriah
Hebrew, meaning 'the Lord is my teacher'.

Morwenna
Welsh, meaning 'maiden'.

Moselle
(alt. Mozell, Mozella, Mozelle)
Hebrew, meaning 'saviour'.

Mulan
Chinese, meaning 'wood orchid'.

Muriel
Irish Gaelic, meaning 'sea-bright'.

Mya
(alt. Myah)
Greek, meaning 'mother'.

Myfanwy
Welsh, meaning 'my little lovely one'.

Myra
Latin, meaning 'scented oil'.

Myrna
(alt. Mirna)
Irish Gaelic, meaning 'tender and beloved'.

Myrtle
Irish, from the shrub of the same name.

M

N Girls' names

Nadia
(alt. Nadya)
Russian, meaning 'hope'.

Nadine
French, meaning 'hope'.

Nahara
Aramaic, meaning 'light'.

Naima
Arabic, meaning 'water nymph'.

Nalani
Hawaiian, meaning 'serenity of the skies'.

Nan
(alt. Nanna, Nannie)
Hebrew, meaning 'grace'.

Nancy
(alt. Nanci, Nancie)
Hebrew, meaning 'grace'.

Nanette
(alt. Nannette)
French, meaning 'grace'.

Naomi
(alt. Naoma, Noemi)
Hebrew, meaning 'pleasant'.

Narcissa
Greek, meaning 'daffodil'.

Nastasia

Greek, meaning 'resurrection'.

Natalie
(alt. Natalee, Natalia, Natalya, Nathalie)

Latin, meaning 'birth day'.

Natasha
(alt. Natasa)

Russian, meaning 'birth day'.

Natividad

Spanish, meaning 'Christmas'.

Neda

English, meaning 'wealthy'.

Nedra

English, meaning 'underground'.

Neema

Swahili, meaning 'born of prosperity'.

Neka

Native American, meaning 'goose'.

Nell
(alt. Nelda, Nell, Nella, Nellie, Nelly)

Shortened form of Eleanor, meaning 'light'.

Nemi

Italian, from the lake of the same name.

Neoma

Greek, meaning 'new moon'.

Nereida

Spanish, meaning 'sea nymph'.

Nerissa

Of Greek origin, meaning 'sea nymph'.

Nettie
(alt. Neta)

Shortened form of Henrietta, meaning 'ruler of the house'.

Neva

Spanish, meaning 'snowy'.

Nevaeh

American, meaning 'heaven'.

N

Niamh
(alt. Neve)
Irish, meaning 'brightness'.

Nicki
(alt. Nicky, Nikki)
Shortened form of Nicola, meaning 'victory of the people'.

Nicola
Greek, meaning 'victory of the people'.

Nicole
(alt. Nichol, Nichole, Nicolette, Nicolle, Nikole)
Greek, meaning 'victory of the people'.

Nidia
Spanish, meaning 'graceful'.

Nigella
Irish Gaelic, meaning 'champion'.

Nikita
Greek, meaning 'unconquered'.

Nila
Egyptian, meaning 'Nile'.

Nilda
German, meaning 'battle woman'.

Nina
Spanish, meaning 'girl'.

Nissa
Hebrew, meaning 'sign'.

Nita
Spanish, meaning 'gracious'.

Nixie
German, meaning 'water sprite'.

Noel
(alt. Noelle)
French, meaning 'Christmas'.

Nola
Irish Gaelic, meaning 'white shoulder'.

Nona
Latin, meaning 'ninth'.

N

Nora
(alt. Norah)

Shortened form of Eleanor, meaning 'light'.

Noreen
(alt. Norine)

Irish, meaning 'light'.

Norma

Latin, meaning 'pattern'.

Normandie
(alt. Normandy)

French, from the province of the same name.

Novia

Latin, meaning 'new'.

Nuala

Irish Gaelic, meaning 'white shoulder'.

Nydia

Latin, meaning 'nest'.

Nysa
(alt. Nyssa)

Greek, meaning 'ambition'.

Names of goddesses

Aphrodite (Love: Greek)
Demeter (Harvest: Greek)
Eos (Dawn: Greek)
Isis (Life: Egyptian)
Kali (Death: Indian)
Lakshmi (Wealth: Indian)
Minerva (Wisdom: Roman)
Nephthys (Death: Egyptian)
Saraswati (Arts: Indian)
Vesta (Hearth: Roman)

O Girls' names

Oceana
(alt. Ocean, Océane, Ocie)
Greek, meaning 'ocean'.

Octavia
Latin, meaning 'eighth'.

Oda
(alt. Odie)
Shortened form of Odessa,
meaning 'long voyage'.

Odele
(alt. Odell)
English, meaning 'woad hill'.

Odelia
Hebrew, meaning 'I will praise
the Lord'.

Odessa
Greek, meaning 'long voyage'.

Odette
(alt. Odetta)
French, meaning 'wealthy'.

Odile
(alt. Odilia)
French, meaning 'prospers in
battle'.

Odina
Feminine form of Odin, from
the Nordic god of the same
name.

Odyssey
Greek, meaning 'long journey'.

Oksana

Russian, meaning 'praise to God'.

Ola

(alt. Olie)

Greek, meaning 'man's defender'.

Olena

(alt. Olene)

Russian, meaning 'light'.

Olga

Russian, meaning 'holy'.

Olivia

(alt. Olivev, Oliviana, Olivié)

Latin, meaning 'olive'.

Ollie

Shortened form of Olivia, meaning 'olive'.

Olwen

Welsh, meaning 'white footprint'.

Olympia

(alt. Olimpia)

Greek, meaning 'from Mount Olympus'.

Oma

(alt. Omie)

Arabic, meaning 'leader'.

Omyra

Latin, meaning 'scented oil'.

Ona

(alt. Onnie)

Shortened form of Oneida, meaning 'long awaited'.

Oneida

Native American, meaning 'long awaited'.

Onyx

Latin, meaning 'veined gem'.

Oona

Irish, meaning 'unity'.

Opal

Sanskrit, meaning 'gem'.

Ophelia

(alt. Ofelia, Ophélie)

Greek, meaning 'help'.

Oprah

Hebrew, meaning 'young deer'.

Ora

Latin, meaning 'prayer'.

Orabela

Latin, meaning 'prayer'.

Oralie
(alt. Oralia)

French, meaning 'golden'.

Orane

French, meaning 'rising'.

Orchid

Greek, from the flower of the same name.

Colour names

Blanche
Coral
Ebony
Fawn
Hazel
Olive
Rose
Scarlett
Sienna
Violet

Oriana
(alt. Oriane)

Latin, meaning 'dawning'.

Orla
(alt. Orlaith, Orly)

Irish Gaelic, meaning 'golden lady'.

Orlean

French, meaning 'plum'.

Orsa
(alt. Osia, Ossie)

Latin, meaning 'bear'.

Otthid

Greek, meaning 'prospers in battle'.

Ottilie
(alt. Ottie)

French, meaning 'prospers in battle'.

Ouida

French, meaning 'renowned in battle'.

Ozette

Native American, from the village of the same name.

O

Popular Scottish names for boys and girls

Aileen
Alastair
Angus
Fergus
Isla
Mac
Malcolm
Rhona
Rossalyn
Saundra

P

Girls' names

Padma
Hindi, meaning 'lotus'.

Paige
(alt. Page)
French, meaning 'serving boy'.

Paisley
Scottish, from the town of the same name.

Palma
(alt. Palmira)
Latin, meaning 'palm tree'.

Paloma
Spanish, meaning 'dove'.

Pam
Shortened form of Pamela, meaning 'all honey'.

Pamela
(alt. Pamala, Pamella, Pamla)
Greek, meaning 'all honey'.

Pandora
Greek, meaning 'all gifted'.

Pangiota
Greek, meaning 'all is holy'.

Pansy
French, from the flower of the same name.

Paradisa
(alt. Paradis)
Greek, meaning 'garden orchard'.

Paris
(alt. Parisa)
Greek, from the mythological hero of the same name.

Parker
English, meaning 'park keeper'.

Parthenia
Greek, meaning 'virginal'.

Parthenope
Greek, from the mythological Siren of the same name.

Parvati
Sanskrit, meaning 'daughter of the mountain'.

Pascale
French, meaning 'Easter'.

Pat
(alt. Patsy, Patti, Pattie, Patty)
Shortened form of Patricia, meaning 'noble'.

Patience
French, meaning 'the state of being patient'.

Patricia
(alt. Patrice)
Latin, meaning 'noble'.

Paula
Latin, meaning 'small'.

Pauline
(alt. Paulette, Paulina)
Latin, meaning 'small'.

Paxton
Latin, meaning 'peaceful town'.

Paz
Spanish, meaning 'peace'.

Pazia
Hebrew, meaning 'golden'.

Peace
English, meaning 'peace'.

Pearl
(alt. Pearle, Pearlie, Perla)
Latin, meaning 'pale gemstone'.

P

Gem and precious stone names

Amber
Crystal
Diamond
Emerald
Garnet
Jade
Opal
Pearl
Ruby

Peggy
(alt. Peggie)
Greek, meaning 'pearl'.

Pelia
Hebrew, meaning 'marvel of God'.

Penelope
Greek, meaning 'bobbin worker'.

Penny
(alt. Penni, Pennie)
Greek, meaning 'bobbin worker'.

Peony
Greek, from the flower of the same name.

Perdita
Latin, meaning 'lost'.

Peri
(alt. Perri)
Hebrew, meaning 'outcome'.

Perry
French, meaning 'pear tree'.

Persephone
Greek, meaning 'bringer of destruction'.

Petra
(alt. Petrina)
Greek, meaning 'rock'.

Petula
Latin, meaning 'to seek'.

Petunia
Greek, from the flower of the same name.

Phaedra
Greek, meaning 'bright'.

303

Philippa

Greek, meaning 'horse lover'.

Philomena
(alt. Philoma)

Greek, meaning 'loved one'.

Phoebe

Greek, meaning 'shining and brilliant'.

Phoenix

Greek, meaning 'red as blood'.

Phyllida

Greek, meaning 'leafy bough'.

Phyllis
(alt. Phillia, Phylis)

Greek, meaning 'leafy bough'.

Pia

Latin, meaning 'pious'.

Pilar

Spanish, meaning 'pillar'.

Piper

English, meaning 'pipe player'.

Pippa

Shortened form of Philippa, meaning 'horse lover'.

Plum

Latin, from the fruit of the same name.

Polly

Hebrew, meaning 'bitter'.

Spelling options

C vs K (Catherine or Katherine)
E vs I (Alex or Alix)
G vs J (Geri or Jerry)
N vs NE (Ann or Anne)
O vs OU (Honor or Honour)
S vs Z (Susie or Suzie)
Y vs IE (Carry or Carrie)

P

Pomona

Latin, meaning 'apple'.

Poppy

Latin, from the flower of the same name.

Portia

(alt. Porsha)

Latin, meaning 'from the Portia clan'.

Posy

English, meaning 'small flower'.

Precious

Latin, meaning 'of great worth'.

Priela

Hebrew, meaning 'fruit of God'.

Primrose

English, meaning 'first rose'.

Princess

English, meaning 'daughter of the monarch'.

Priscilla

(alt. Prisca, Priscila)

Latin, meaning 'ancient'.

Priya

Hindi, meaning 'loved one'.

Prudence

Latin, meaning 'caution'.

Prudie

Shortened form of Prudence, meaning 'caution'.

Prunella

Latin, meaning 'small plum'.

Psyche

Greek, meaning 'breath'.

P

Girls' names

Qiturah
Arabic, meaning 'incense'.

Queen
(alt. Queenie)
English, meaning 'queen'.

Quiana
American, meaning 'silky'.

Quincy
(alt. Quincey)
French, meaning 'estate of the fifth son'.

Quinn
Irish Gaelic, meaning 'counsel'.

Foreign alternatives

Eleanor – Elenora, Elinor
Helen – Galina, Helene
Margaret – Gretel, Marguerite, Marjorie
Sarah – Sara, Sarine, Zara
Violet – Iolanthe

No-nickname names

April
Beth
Dana
Joy
Jude
June
Karen
May

R Girls' names

Rachel
(alt. Rachael, Rachelle)
Hebrew, meaning 'ewe'.

Radhika
Sanskrit, meaning 'prosperous'.

Rae
(alt. Ray)
Shortened form of Rachel,
meaning 'ewe'.

Rahima
Arabic, meaning
'compassionate'.

Raina
(alt. Rain, Raine, Rainey, Rayne)
Latin, meaning 'queen'.

Raissa
(alt. Raisa)
Yiddish, meaning 'rose'.

Raleigh
(alt. Rayleigh)
English, meaning 'meadow of
roe deer'.

Rama
(alt. Ramey, Ramya)
Hebrew, meaning 'exalted'.

Ramona
(alt. Romona)
Spanish, meaning 'wise
guardian'.

R

Rana
(alt. Rania, Rayna)

Arabic, meaning 'beautiful thing'.

Randy
(alt. Randi)

Shortened form of Miranda, meaning 'admirable'.

Rani
Sanskrit, meaning 'queen'.

Raphaela
(alt. Rafaela, Raffaella)

Spanish, meaning 'healing God'.

Raquel
(alt. Racquel)

Hebrew, meaning 'ewe'.

Rashida
Turkish, meaning 'righteous'.

Raven
(alt. Ravyn)

English, from the bird of the same name.

Razia
Arabic, meaning 'contented'.

Reagan
(alt. Reagen, Regan)

Irish Gaelic, meaning 'descendant of Riagán'.

Reba
Shortened form of Rebecca, meaning 'joined'.

Rebecca
(alt. Rebekah)

Hebrew, meaning 'joined'.

Reese
Welsh, meaning 'fiery and zealous'.

Regina
Latin, meaning 'queen'.

Reina
(alt. Reyna, Rheyna)

Spanish, meaning 'queen'.

Rena
(alt. Reena)

Hebrew, meaning 'serene'.

Renata
Latin, meaning 'reborn'.

Rene

Greek, meaning 'peace'.

Renée

(alt. Renae)

French, meaning 'reborn'.

Renita

Latin, meaning 'resistant'.

Reshma

(alt. Resha)

Sanskrit, meaning 'silk'.

Reta

(alt. Retha, Retta)

Shortened form of Margaret, meaning 'pearl'.

Rhea

Greek, meaning 'earth'.

Rheta

Greek, meaning 'eloquent speaker'.

Rhiannon

(alt. Reanna, Reanne, Rhian, Rhianna)

Welsh, meaning 'witch'.

Rhoda

Greek, meaning 'rose'.

Rhona

Nordic, meaning 'rough island'.

Rhonda

(alt. Ronda)

Welsh, meaning 'noisy'.

Ría

(alt. Rie, Riya)

Shortened form of Victoria, meaning 'victor'.

Ricki

(alt. Rieko, Rika, Rikki)

Shortened form of Frederica, meaning 'peaceful ruler'.

Riley

Irish Gaelic, meaning 'courageous'.

Rilla

German, meaning 'small brook'.

Rima

Arabic, meaning 'antelope'.

R

Riona

Irish Gaelic, meaning 'like a queen'.

Ripley

English, meaning 'shouting man's meadow'.

Risa

Latin, meaning 'laughter'.

Rita

Shortened form of Margaret, meaning 'pearl'.

River

(alt. Riviera)

English, from the body of water of the same name.

Robbie

(alt. Robi, Roby)

Shortened form of Roberta, meaning 'bright flame'.

Roberta

English, meaning 'bright flame'.

Robin

(alt. Robbin, Robyn)

English, meaning 'bright flame'.

Rochelle

(alt. Richelle, Rochel)

French, meaning 'little rock'.

Rogue

French, meaning 'beggar'.

Rohina

(alt. Rohini)

Sanskrit, meaning 'sandalwood'.

Roisin

Irish Gaelic, meaning 'bright flame'.

Rolanda

German, meaning 'famous land'.

Roma

Italian, meaning 'Rome'.

Romaine

(alt. Romina)

French, meaning 'from Rome'.

Romola

(alt. Romilda, Romily)

Latin, meaning 'Roman woman'.

R

'Powerful' names

Allura
Aubrey
Inga
Isis
Lenna
Ulrika

Romy

Shortened form of Rosemary, meaning 'dew of the sea'.

Rona

(alt. Ronia, Ronja, Ronna)

Nordic, meaning 'rough island'.

Ronnie

(alt. Roni)

English, meaning 'strong counsel'.

Rosa

Italian, meaning 'rose'.

Rosabel

(alt. Rosabella)

Contraction of Rose and Belle, meaning 'beautiful rose'.

Rosalie

(alt. Rosale, Rosalia, Rosalina)

French, meaning 'rose garden'.

Rosalind

(alt. Rosalinda)

Spanish, meaning 'pretty rose'.

Rosalyn

(alt. Rosaleen, Rosaline, Roselyn)

Contraction of Rose and Lynn, meaning 'pretty rose'.

Rosamond

(alt. Rosamund)

German, meaning 'renowned protector'.

Rose

Latin, from the flower of the same name.

Roseanne

(alt. Rosana, Rosann, Rosanna, Rosanne, Roseann, Roseanna)

Contraction of Rose and Anne, meaning 'graceful rose'.

Rosemary

(alt. Rosemarie)

Latin, meaning 'dew of the sea'.

R

Rosie
(alt. Rosia)

Shortened form of Rosemary, meaning 'dew of the sea'.

Rosita

Spanish, meaning 'rose'.

Rowena
(alt. Rowan)

Welsh, meaning 'slender and fair'.

Roxanne
(alt. Roxana, Roxane, Roxanna)

Persian, meaning 'dawn'.

Roxie

Shortened form of Roxanne, meaning 'dawn'.

Rubena
(alt. Rubina)

Hebrew, meaning 'behold, a son'.

Ruby
(alt. Rubi, Rubie)

English, meaning 'red gemstone'.

Ruth
(alt. Ruthe, Ruthie)

Hebrew, meaning 'friend and companion'.

Popular South American names for boys and girls

Atl
Centehua
Citlali
Coatl
Eréndira
Itzli
Matlal
Teiuc
Xochitl
Zolin

R

S Girls' names

Saba
(alt. Sabah)
Greek, meaning 'from Sheba'.

Sabina
(alt. Sabine)
Latin, meaning 'from the Sabine tribe'.

Sabrina
Latin, meaning 'the River Severn'.

Sadie
(alt. Sade, Sadye)
Hebrew, meaning 'princess'.

Saffron
English, from the spice of the same name.

Safiya
Arabic, meaning 'sincere friend'.

Sage
(alt. Saga, Saige)
Latin, meaning 'wise and healthy'.

Sahara
Arabic, meaning 'desert'.

Sakura
Japanese, meaning 'cherry blossom'.

Sally
(alt. Sallie)
Hebrew, meaning 'princess'.

S

Salome
(alt. Salma)
Hebrew, meaning 'peace'.

Sam
(alt. Sammie, Sammy)
Shortened form of Samantha, meaning 'told by God'.

Samantha
Hebrew, meaning 'told by God'.

Samara
(alt. Samaria, Samira)
Hebrew, meaning 'under God's rule'.

Sanaa
Arabic, meaning 'brilliance'.

Sandra
(alt. Saundra)
Shortened form of Alexandra, meaning 'defender of mankind'.

Sandy
(alt. Sandi)
Shortened form of Sandra, meaning 'defender of mankind'.

Sangeeta
Hindi, meaning 'musical'.

Sanna
(alt. Saniya, Sanne, Sanni)
Hebrew, meaning 'lily'.

Santana
(alt. Santina)
Spanish, meaning 'holy'.

Sapphire
(alt. Saphira)
Hebrew, meaning 'blue gemstone'.

Sarah
(alt. Sara, Sarai, Sariah)
Hebrew, meaning 'princess'.

Sasha
(alt. Sacha, Sascha)
Russian, meaning 'man's defender'.

Saskia
(alt. Saskie)
Dutch, meaning 'the Saxon people'.

S

Savannah
(alt. Savanah, Savanna, Savina)
Spanish, meaning 'treeless'.

Scarlett
(alt. Scarlet)
English, meaning 'scarlet'.

Scout
French, meaning 'to listen'.

Sedona
(alt. Sedna)
Spanish, from the city of the same name.

Selah
(alt Sela)
Hebrew, meaning 'cliff'.

Selby
English, meaning 'manor village'.

Selena
(alt. Salena, Salima, Salina, Selene, Selina)
Greek, meaning 'moon goddess'.

Selma
German, meaning 'Godly helmet'.

Seneca
Native American, meaning 'from the Seneca tribe'.

Sephora
Hebrew, meaning 'bird'.

September
Latin, meaning 'seventh month'.

Seraphina
(alt. Serafina, Seraphia, Seraphine)
Hebrew, meaning 'ardent'.

Serena
(alt. Sarina, Sereana)
Latin, meaning 'tranquil'.

Serenity
Latin, meaning 'serene'.

Shania
(alt. Shaina, Shana, Shaniya)
Hebrew, meaning 'beautiful'.

S

Shanice

American, meaning 'from Africa'.

Shaniqua
(alt. Shanika)

African, meaning 'warrior princess'.

Shanna

English, meaning 'old'.

Shannon
(alt. Shannan, Shanon)

Irish Gaelic, meaning 'old and ancient'.

Shantal
(alt. Shantel, Shantell)

French, from the place of the same name.

Shanti

Hindi, meaning 'peaceful'.

Sharlene

German, meaning 'man'.

Sharon
(alt. Sharen, Sharona, Sharron, Sharyn)

Hebrew, meaning 'a plain'.

Spring names

April
Cerelia
Kelda
May
Primavera
Verda
Verna

Shasta

American, from the mountain of the same name.

Shauna
(alt. Shawna)

Irish, meaning 'the Lord is gracious'.

Shayla
(alt. Shaylie, Shayna, Sheyla)

Irish, meaning 'blind'.

Shea

Irish Gaelic, meaning 'from the fairy fort'.

Sheena

Irish, meaning 'the Lord is gracious'.

S

Sheila
(alt. Shelia)

Irish, meaning 'blind'.

Shelby
(alt. Shelba, Shelbie)

English, meaning 'estate on the ledge'.

Shelley
(alt. Shelli, Shellie, Shelly)

English, meaning 'meadow on the ledge'.

Shenandoah

Native American, meaning 'after an Oneida chief'.

Sheridan

Irish Gaelic, meaning 'wild man'.

Sherry
(alt. Sheree, Sheri, Sherie, Sherri, Sherrie)

Shortened form of Cheryl, meaning 'man'.

Sheryl
(alt. Sherryl)

German, meaning 'man'.

Shiloh

Hebrew, from the Biblical place of the same name.

Shirley
(alt. Shirlee)

English, meaning 'bright meadow'.

Shivani

Sanskrit, meaning 'wife of Shiva'.

Shona

Irish Gaelic, meaning 'God is gracious'.

Shoshana
(alt. Shoshanna)

Hebrew, meaning 'lily'.

Shura

Russian, meaning 'man's defender'.

Sian
(alt. Sianna)

Welsh, meaning 'the Lord is gracious'.

S

Sibyl
(alt. Sybil)
Greek, meaning 'seer and oracle'.

Sidney
(alt. Sydney)
English, meaning 'from St Denis'.

Sidonie
(alt. Sidonia, Sidony)
Latin, meaning 'from Sidonia'.

Siena
(alt. Sienna)
Latin, from the town of the same name.

Sierra
Spanish, meaning 'saw'.

Signa
(alt. Signe)
Scandinavian, meaning 'victory'.

Sigrid
Nordic, meaning 'fair victory'.

Silja
Scandinavian, meaning 'blind'.

Simcha
Hebrew, meaning 'joy'.

Simone
(alt. Simona)
Hebrew, meaning 'listening intently'.

Sinead
Irish, meaning 'the Lord is gracious'.

Siobhan
Irish, meaning 'the Lord is gracious'.

Siren
(alt. Sirena)
Greek, meaning 'entangler'.

Siria
Spanish, meaning 'glowing'.

Skye
(alt. Sky)
Scottish, from the island of the same name.

Skyler
(alt. Skyla, Skylar)
Dutch, meaning 'giving shelter'.

S

Sloane
(alt. *Sloan*)
Irish Gaelic, meaning 'man of arms'.

Socorro
Spanish, meaning 'to aid'.

Sojourner
English, meaning 'temporary stay'.

Solana
Spanish, meaning 'sunlight'.

Solange
French, meaning 'with dignity'.

Soledad
Spanish, meaning 'solitude'.

Soleil
French, meaning 'sun'.

Solveig
Scandinavian, meaning 'woman of the house'.

Sonia
(alt. *Sonja, Sonya*)
Greek, meaning 'wisdom'.

Sophia
(alt. *Sofia, Sofie, Sophie*)
Greek, meaning 'wisdom'.

Sophronia
Greek, meaning 'sensible'.

Soraya
Persian, meaning 'princess'.

Sorcha
Irish Gaelic, meaning 'bright and shining'.

Sorrel
English, from the herb of the same name.

Stacey
(alt. *Stacie, Stacy*)
Greek, meaning 'resurrection'.

Star
(alt. *Starla, Starr*)
English, meaning 'star'.

Stella
Latin, meaning 'star'.

S

Stephanie
(alt. Stefanie, Stephani, Stephania, Stephany)
Greek, meaning 'crowned'.

Sue
(alt. Susie, Suzy)
Shortened form of Susan, meaning 'lily'.

Sukey
(alt. Sukey, Sukie)
Shortened form of Susan, meaning 'lily'.

Summer
English, from the season of the same name.

Sunday
English, meaning 'the first day'.

Sunny
(alt. Sun)
English, meaning 'of a pleasant temperament'.

Suri
Persian, meaning 'red rose'.

Surya
Hindi, from the god of the same name.

Susan
(alt. Susann, Suzan)
Hebrew, meaning 'lily'.

Susannah
(alt. Susana, Susanna, Susanne, Suzanna, Suzanne)
Hebrew, meaning 'lily'.

Svetlana
Russian, meaning 'star'.

Swanhild
Saxon, meaning 'battle swan'.

Sylvia
(alt. Silvia, Sylvie)
Latin, meaning 'from the forest'.

Summer names

August
June
Natsumi
Persephone
Soleil
Summer
Suvi

S

T

Girls' names

Tabitha
(alt. Tabatha)
Aramaic, meaning 'gazelle'.

Tahira
Arabic, meaning 'virginal'.

Tai
Chinese, meaning 'big'.

Taima
(alt. Taina)
Native American, meaning
'peal of thunder'.

Talia
(alt. Tali)
Hebrew, meaning 'heaven's
dew'.

Taliesin
Welsh, meaning 'shining brow'.

Talise
(alt. Talyse)
Native American, meaning
'lovely water'.

Talitha
Aramaic, meaning 'young girl'.

Tallulah
(alt. Taliyah)
Native American, meaning
'leaping water'.

Tamara
(alt. Tamera)
Hebrew, meaning 'palm tree'.

Tamatha
(alt. Tametha)

American, meaning 'dear Tammy'.

Tamika
(alt. Tameka)

American, meaning 'people'.

Tammy
(alt. Tami, Tammie)

Shortened form of Tamsin, meaning 'twin'.

Tamsin

Hebrew, meaning 'twin'.

Tanis

Spanish, meaning 'to make famous'.

Tanya
(alt. Tania, Tanya, Tonya)

Shortened form of Tatiana, meaning 'from the Tatius clan'.

Tara
(alt. Tarah, Tera)

Irish Gaelic, meaning 'rocky hill'.

Tasha
(alt. Taisha, Tarsha)

Shortened form of Natasha, meaning 'Christmas'.

Tatiana
(alt. Tayana)

Russian, meaning 'from the Tatius clan'.

Tatum

English, meaning 'light-hearted'.

Tawny
(alt. Tawanaa, Tawnee, Tawnya)

English, meaning 'golden brown'.

Taya

Greek, meaning 'poor one'.

Taylor
(alt. Tayler)

English, meaning 'tailor'.

Tea

Greek, meaning 'goddess'.

T

Teagan
(alt. Teague, Tegan)
Irish Gaelic, meaning 'poet'.

Teal
English, from the bird of the same name.

Tecla
Greek, meaning 'fame of God'.

Temperance
English, meaning 'virtue'.

Tempest
French, meaning 'storm'.

Teresa
(alt. Terese, Tereza, Theresa, Therese)
Greek, meaning 'harvest'.

Terry
(alt. Teri, Terrie)
Shortened form of Teresa, meaning 'harvest'.

Tessa
(alt. Tess, Tessie)
Shortened form of Teresa, meaning 'harvest'.

Thais
Greek, from the mythological heroine of the same name.

Thalia
Greek, meaning 'blooming'.

Thandi
(alt. Thana)
Arabic, meaning 'thanksgiving'.

Thea
Greek, meaning 'goddess'.

Theda
German, meaning 'people'.

Thelma
Greek, meaning 'will'.

Theodora
Greek, meaning 'gift of God'.

Theodosia
Greek, meaning 'gift of God'.

Thisbe
Greek, from the mythological heroine of the same name.

T

Thomasina

(alt. Thomasin, Thomasine, Thomasyn)

Greek, meaning 'twin'.

Thora

Scandinavian, meaning 'Thor's struggle'.

Tia

(alt. Tiana)

Spanish, meaning 'aunt'.

Tiara

Latin, meaning 'jewelled headband'.

Tierney

Irish Gaelic, meaning 'Lord'.

Tierra

(alt. Tiera)

Spanish, meaning 'land'.

Tiffany

(alt. Tiffani, Tiffanie)

Greek, meaning 'God's appearance'.

Tiggy

Shortened form of Tigris, meaning 'tiger'.

Tigris

Irish Gaelic, meaning 'tiger'.

Tilda

Shortened form of Matilda, meaning 'battle-mighty'.

Tillie

(alt. Tilly)

Shortened form of Matilda, meaning 'battle-mighty'.

Timothea

Greek, meaning 'honouring God'.

Tina

(alt. Teena, Tena)

Shortened form of Christina, meaning 'anointed Christian'.

Tirion

Welsh, meaning 'kind and gentle'.

Tirzah

Hebrew, meaning 'pleasantness'.

Titania

Greek, meaning 'giant'.

Toby
(alt. Tobi)
Hebrew, meaning 'God is good'.

Toni
(alt. Tony)
Latin, meaning 'invaluable'.

Tonia
(alt. Tonja, Tonya)
Russian, meaning 'praiseworthy'.

Topaz
Latin, meaning 'golden gemstone'.

Tori
(alt. Tora)
Shortened form of Victoria, meaning 'victory'.

Autumn names

Autumn
Demetria
September
Theresa
Tracey

Tova
(alt. Tovah, Tove)
Hebrew, meaning 'good'.

Tracy
(alt. Tracey, Tracie)
Greek, meaning 'harvest'.

Treva
Welsh, meaning 'homestead'.

Tricia
Shortened form of Patricia, meaning 'aristocratic'.

Trilby
English, meaning 'vocal trills'.

Trina
(alt. Trena)
Greek, meaning 'pure'.

Trinity
Latin, meaning 'triad'.

Trisha
Shortened form of Patricia, meaning 'noble'.

Trista
Latin, meaning 'sad'.

Trixie

Shortened form of Beatrix, meaning 'bringer of gladness'.

Trudy
(alt. *Tru, Trudie*)

Shortened form of Gertrude, meaning 'strength of a spear'.

Tullia

Spanish, meaning 'bound for glory'.

Twyla
(alt. *Twila*)

American, meaning 'star'.

Tyler

English, meaning 'tiler'.

Tyra

Scandinavian, meaning 'Thor's struggle'.

Tzipporah

Hebrew, meaning 'bird'.

Popular Spanish names for boys and girls

Carmen
Catalina
Diego
Esmeralda
Jesus
Jose
Juanita
Miguel
Ramona
Santiago

T

U

Girls' names

Ula
(alt. Ulla)
Celtic, meaning 'gem of the sea'.

Ulrika
(alt. Urica)
German, meaning 'power of the wolf'.

Uma
Sanskrit, meaning 'flax'.

Una
Latin, meaning 'one'.

Undine
Latin, meaning 'little wave'.

Winter names

January
Neva
Neve
Perdita
Rainer
Tahoma

Unice
Greek, meaning ' victorious'.

Unique
Latin, meaning 'only one'.

Unity
English, meaning 'oneness'.

Uriela

Hebrew, meaning 'God's light'.

Ursula

Latin, meaning 'little female bear'.

Uta

German, meaning 'prospers in battle'.

 Girls' names

Vada

German, meaning 'famous ruler'.

Vale

Shortened form of Valencia, meaning 'strong and healthy'.

Valencia

(alt. Valancy, Valarece)

Latin, meaning 'strong and healthy'.

Valentina

Latin, meaning 'strong and healthy'.

Valentine

Latin, from the saint of the same name.

Valeria

Latin, meaning 'to be healthy and strong'.

Valerie

(alt. Valarie, Valery, Valorie)

Latin, meaning 'to be healthy and strong'.

Valia

(alt. Vallie)

Shortened form of Valerie, meaning 'to be healthy and strong'.

Vandana

Sanskrit, meaning 'worship'.

Vanessa
(alt. Vanesa)

English, from the *Gulliver's Travels* character of the same name.

Vanity

Latin, meaning 'self-obsessed'.

Vashti

Persian, meaning 'beauty'.

Veda

Sanskrit, meaning 'knowledge and wisdom'.

Vega

Arabic, meaning 'falling vulture'.

Velda

German, meaning 'ruler'.

Vella

American, meaning 'beautiful'.

Velma

English, meaning 'determined protector'.

Venice
(alt. Venetia, Venita)

Latin, from the city of the same name.

Venus

Latin, from the Roman goddess of the same name.

Vera
(alt. Verla, Verlie)

Slavic, meaning 'faith'.

Verda
(alt. Verdie)

Latin, meaning 'spring-like'.

Verena

Latin, meaning 'true'.

Verity

Latin, meaning 'truth'.

Verna
(alt. Vernie)

Latin, meaning 'spring green'.

Verona

Latin, from the city of the same name.

Christmas names

Carol
Eve
Gloria
Holly
Ivy
Mary
Natasha
Noël
Robin

Veronica
(alt. Verica, Veronique)
Latin, meaning 'true image'.

Veruca
Latin, meaning 'wart'.

Vesta
Latin, from the Roman goddess of the same name.

Vicenta
Latin, meaning 'prevailing'.

Vicky
(alt. Vicki, Vickie, Vikki, Vix)
Shortened form of Victoria, meaning 'victory'.

Victoria
Latin, meaning 'victory'.

Vida
Spanish, meaning 'life'.

Vidya
Sanskrit, meaning 'knowledge'.

Vienna
Latin, from the city of the same name.

Vigdis
Scandinavian, meaning 'war goddess'.

Vina
(alt. Vena)
Spanish, meaning 'vineyard'.

Viola
Latin, meaning 'violet'.

Violet
(alt. Violetta)
Latin, meaning 'purple'.

Virgie
Shortened form of Virginia, meaning 'maiden'.

V

333

Virginia
(alt. Virginie)

Latin, meaning 'maiden'.

Vita

Latin, meaning 'life'.

Vittoria

Variation of Victoria, meaning 'victory'.

Viva

Latin, meaning 'alive'.

Viveca

Scandinavian, meaning 'war fortress'.

Vivian
(alt. Vivien, Vivienne)

Latin, meaning 'lively'.

Vonda

Czech, meaning 'from the tribe of Vandals'.

Food-inspired names

Anise
Candy
Cherry
Coco
Ginger
Honey
Meena
Olive
Saffron

Girls' names

Waleska
Polish, meaning 'beautiful'.

Wallis
English, meaning 'from Wales'.

Wanda
(alt. Waneta, Wanita)
Slavic, meaning 'tribe of the vandals'.

Waneta
Variation of Wanda meaning 'tribe of the vandals'.

Wanita
Variation of Wanda meaning 'tribe of the vandals'.

Wava
English, meaning 'way'.

Waverly
Old English, meaning 'meadow of aspens'.

Wendy
English, meaning 'friend'.

Whisper
English, meaning 'whisper'.

Whitley
Old English, meaning 'white meadow'.

Whitney
Old English, meaning 'white island'.

Wilda

German, meaning 'willow tree'.

Wilhelmina

German, meaning 'will-helmet'.

Willene
(alt. Willia)

German, meaning 'helmet'.

Willow

English, from the tree of the same name.

Wilma

German, meaning 'protection'.

Winifred

Old English, meaning 'holy and blessed'.

Winnie

Shortened form of Winifred, meaning 'holy and blessed'.

Winona
(alt. Wynona)

Indian, meaning 'first born daughter'.

Winslow

English, meaning 'friend's hill'.

Winter

English, meaning 'winter'.

Wisteria

English, meaning 'flower'.

Wren

English, meaning 'wren'.

Wynne

Welsh, meaning 'white'.

Bird names

Ava
Oriole
Raven
Teal
Wren

W

 Girls' names

Xanthe
(alt. Xanthe)
Greek, meaning 'blonde'.

Xanthippe
Greek, meaning 'nagging'.

Xaverie
Greek, meaning 'bright'.

Xaviera
Arabic, meaning 'bright'.

Xena
Greek, meaning 'foreigner'.

Xenia
Greek, meaning 'foreigner'.

Ximena
Greek, meaning 'listening'.

Xiomara
Spanish, meaning 'battle-ready'.

Xochitl
Spanish, meaning 'flower'.

Xoey
Variation of Zoe, meaning 'life'.

Xristina
Variation of Christina, meaning 'follower of Christ'.

Xylia
(alt. Xylina, Xyloma)
Greek, meaning 'from the woods'.

Popular Welsh names for boys and girls

Bronwen
Cerys
Dylan
Gwynn
Ioan
Myfanwy
Owain
Padraig
Rhys
Siân

Girls' names

Yadira
Arabic, meaning 'worthy'.

Yael
Hebrew, meaning 'mountain goat'.

Yaffa
(alt. Yahaira, Yajaira)
Hebrew, meaning lovely.

Yamilet
Arabic, meaning 'beautiful'.

Yana
Hebrew, meaning 'the Lord is gracious'.

Yanira
Hawaiian, meaning 'pretty'.

Yareli
Latin, meaning 'golden'.

Yaretzi
(alt. Yaritza)
Hawaiian, meaning 'forever beloved'.

Yasmin
(alt. Yasmeen, Yasmina)
Persian, meaning 'jasmine flower'.

Yelena
Greek, meaning 'bright and chosen'.

Yesenia
Arabic, meaning 'flower'.

Yetta

English, from Henrietta, meaning 'ruler of the house'.

Yeva

Hebrew variant of Eve, meaning 'life'.

Ylva

Old Norse, meaning 'sea wolf'.

Yoki
(alt. Yoko)

Native American, meaning 'rain'.

Yolanda
(alt. Yolonda)

Spanish, meaning 'violet flower'.

Yoselin

English, meaning 'lovely'.

Yoshiko

Japanese, meaning 'good child'.

Ysabel

English, meaning 'God's promise'.

Names from nature

Acacia
Amaryllis
Dahlia
Juniper
Primrose

Ysanne

Contraction of Isabel and Anne.

Yuki

Japanese, meaning 'lucky'.

Yuliana

Latin, meaning 'youthful'.

Yuridia

Russian, meaning 'farmer'.

Yvette
(alt. Yvonne)

French, meaning 'yew'.

Z Girls' names

Zafira

Arabic, meaning 'successful'.

Zahara

(alt. Zahava, Zahra)

Arabic, meaning 'flowering and shining'.

Zaida

(alt. Zaide)

Arabic, meaning 'prosperous'.

Zalika

Swahili, meaning 'well born'.

Zaltana

Arabic, meaning 'high mountain'.

Zamia

Greek, meaning 'pine cone'.

Zaniyah

Arabic, meaning 'lily'.

Zara

(alt. Zaria, Zariah, Zora)

Arabic, meaning 'radiance'.

Zelda

German, meaning 'dark battle'.

Zelia

(alt. Zella)

Scandinavian, meaning 'sunshine'.

Zelma

German, meaning 'helmet'.

Zemirah

Hebrew, meaning 'joyous melody'.

Zena
(alt. Zenia, Zina)
Greek, meaning 'hospitable'.

Zenaida
Greek, meaning 'the life of Zeus'.

Zenobia
Latin, meaning 'the life of Zeus'.

Zetta
Italian, meaning 'Z'.

Zia
Arabic, meaning 'light and splendour'.

Zinaida
Greek, meaning 'belonging to Zeus'.

Zinnia
Latin, meaning 'flower'.

Zipporah
Hebrew, meaning 'bird'.

Zita
(alt. Ziva)
Spanish, meaning 'little girl'.

Zoe
Greek, meaning 'life'.

Zoila
Greek, meaning 'life'.

Zoraida
Spanish, meaning 'captivating woman'.

Zosia
(alt. Zosima)
Greek, meaning 'wisdom'.

Zoya
Greek, meaning 'life'.

Zula
African, meaning 'brilliant'.

Zuleika
Arabic, meaning 'fair and intelligent'.

Zulma
Arabic, meaning 'peace'.

Zuzana
Hebrew, meaning 'lily'.

Zuzu
Czech, meaning 'flower'.

Z

whiteLADDER

the parenting & family health experts

Get 30% off your next purchase...

We are publishers of a growing **parenting and family health** range of books. We pride ourselves on our friendly and accessible approach whilst providing you with sensible, non-preachy information. This is what makes us **different from other publishers**.

And we are keen to **find out what you think** about our book.

If you love this book **tell us why** and tell your friends. And if you think we could do better, **let us know**. Your thoughts and opinions are important to us and help us produce the best books we possibly can.

As a **thank you** we'll give you 30% off your next purchase. Write to us at **info@whiteladderpress.co.uk** and we'll send you an online voucher by return.

  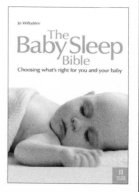

Come and visit us at **www.whiteladderpress.co.uk**